"When it comes to investing finan̲_____
cultural partnerships, there are vast opportunities to build God's kingdom. There is also an array of thorny tensions about money, arising mainly from cultural misunderstanding. Mary Lederleitner has done a great job of affirming the opportunities and navigating the cultural tensions. At last, here is a readable book with careful biblical insight about money and partnership, with gleanings from leading missiologists and expert partnership practitioners. Mixed in are real-life stories of partnership failures and great successes. *Cross-Cultural Partnerships* is an essential resource for Christian mission in the twenty-first century."

Werner Mischke, vice president, Mission One

"From years of experience working with NGOs in a number of countries around the world, Mary Lederleitner writes knowledgeably about the strains that differences in worldview and in cultural expectations regarding accountability in handling money can place on mission partnerships, themselves entered into with the best of intentions. This book is practical, well focused and vision-expanding. I recommend it highly."

Dwight P. Baker, associate director and associate editor, *International Bulletin of Missionary Research*, Overseas Ministries Study Center

"Over the years Mary's insights into the world of missions have informed, challenged and delighted me. Her organizational awareness, hands-on field experience and heart for others provide a 360° perspective on cross-cultural partnerships. This book is a tremendous resource for churches, mission agencies and any who wish to develop international partnerships."

Adele Calhoun, copastor, Redeemer Community Church, and author of *Spiritual Disciplines Handbook*

"I began reading *Cross-Cultural Partnerships* and became practically glued to it! Its case studies enlarge my own understanding of the issues. This book will contribute to better beliefs and practices regarding the proper place of money in kingdom partnerships."

Alex Araujo, director of new mission initiatives, Partners International

"Money is the defining and dividing issue in cross-cultural partnerships, and Mary Lederleitner has given us the essential cultural insights and very practical tools and applications to navigate these treacherous waters. Writing from years of experience, Mary shines light on our harmful assumptions and then guides us to better and biblical ways to achieve accountability, build capacity and create sustainable partnerships with lasting impact for the kingdom of God. This very compact book is a must for everyone who aspires to partner with Majority World leaders and churches. Its fresh insights and applications make it invaluable as a training tool, one that I will use in seminars for Western and Majority World church and mission leaders."

Sherwood Lingenfelter, provost and senior vice president, Fuller Theological Seminary, and author of *Ministering Cross-Culturally*

"Mary Lederleitner's conversational style combined with her fair-minded approach creates a book that is friendly as well as informative about a tough subject. She wastes no time pointing out the gorilla in the room when it comes to money in cross-cultural partnerships—cultural differences. Important as it is, culture is no excuse for bad behavior, and she tackles that as well with helpful material on how to prevent and detect embezzlement and fraud. If you read only one of the few books on money in mission partnerships, read this one."

Daniel Rickett, author of *Making Your Partnership Work* and *Building Strategic Relationships*

"In our globalized world the North American missions community needs *Cross-Cultural Partnerships!* I found it filled with practical, down-to-earth advice built on extensive experience and solid research. Mary is much more than just an accountant with a decade of living experience working through issues of partnering with others; she truly knows how to compassionately listen, apply what she learns to test it out and then pass it on to the rest of us in ways that will benefit the whole body of Christ."

Scott Moreau, professor of missions and intercultural studies, Wheaton College Graduate School, and author of *Introducing World Missions*

"Mary takes us straight to the intersection of mission, money, culture and partnerships. She walks us through key issues regarding money that can complicate, derail and even destroy cross-cultural partnerships. Using biblical perspectives, categories from anthropology and practical experience, she provides valuable guidance. This is a must-read for anyone struggling with the role of money in such contexts."

John Watters, former executive director, Wycliffe Bible Translators International

"Mary has done an incredible job in storying, through numerous case studies, the wedding as well as the marriage of good accountability and good cultural relationship. . . . I commend the grace and boldness given to her to put this together. It is a worthy work, because money matters a lot in mission. I enjoyed reading it, perhaps because there are so many true-life stories in virtually every chapter. I extol this work joyfully to the body of Christ worldwide as an unbiased, well-set-out and constructively presented view on money and global Christianity. I will particularly love to have numerous copies to give to missions leaders in Africa while recommending it for use in field preparatory trainings."

Timothy O. Olonade, executive secretary, Nigeria Evangelical Missions Association (NEMA)

"*Cross-Cultural Partnerships* brings the rare combination of mind, heart and experience of a seasoned yet compassionate accountability expert who is also a missionary with extensive field experience. Its realistic portrayal of the issues and practical suggestions for policy and action make this an invaluable read for anyone wanting to address one of the critical, central issues in partnerships within the growing global church."

Phill Butler, director, Vision Synergy, and author of *Well Connected: Releasing Power, Restoring Hope Through Kingdom Partnerships*

"In matters of money, American evangelical mission has certainly made a mark in many positive ways, but our methodology in applying the funds has not always made such a positive mark. In this volume, Mary Lederleitner pulls some of those skeletons out of our dusty closets for a fresh examination of what we did right and what we could have done better. She offers many practical ways to avoid pitfalls as we move toward a more globalized mission partnership in the twenty-first century."

Gilles Gravelle, director of research and field project development, The Seed Company

Cross-Cultural Partnerships

Navigating the Complexities

of Money and Mission

MARY T. LEDERLEITNER

Foreword by DUANE H. ELMER

IVP Books

An imprint of InterVarsity Press
Downers Grove, Illinois

InterVarsity Press
P.O. Box 1400, Downers Grove, IL 60515-1426
World Wide Web: www.ivpress.com
E-mail: email@ivpress.com

InterVarsity Press® is the book-publishing division of InterVarsity Christian Fellowship/USA®, a
movement of students and faculty active on campus at hundreds of universities, colleges and schools
of nursing in the United States of America, and a member movement of the International Fellowship
of Evangelical Students. For information about local and regional activities, write Public Relations
Dept., InterVarsity Christian Fellowship/USA, 6400 Schroeder Rd., P.O. Box 7895, Madison, WI
53707-7895, or visit the IVCF website at <www.intervarsity.org>.

All Scripture quotations, unless otherwise indicated, are taken from the New American Standard
Bible®, copyright 1960, 1962, 1963, 1968, 1971, 1972, 1973, 1975, 1977, 1995 by The Lockman
Foundation. Used by permission.

Design: Cindy Kiple
Images: Bryce Flynn Photography, Inc./Getty Images

ISBN 978-0-8308-3747-2

Printed in the United States of America ∞

Library of Congress Cataloging-in-Publication Data

Lederleitner, Mary T., 1963-
  Cross-cultural partnerships: navigating the complexities of money
and mission / Mary T. Lederleitner; foreword by Duane H. Elmer.
     p. cm.
  Includes bibliographical references (p.   )
  ISBN 978-0-8308-3747-2 (pbk.: alk. paper)
  1. Missions—Finance. 2. International cooperation. I. Title.
  BV2081.L44 2010
  266.0068'1—dc22
                                                          2009048953

P   18   17   16   15   14   13   12   11   10   9   8   7   6   5   4   3   2

Y   25   24   23   22   21   20   19   18   17   16   15   14   13   12   11

This book is dedicated to the countless missionaries and indigenous leaders I have met over the years. Whether expatriate staff or working within their own national borders, they have inspired me to the depths of my being. They truly are my modern-day "heroes of faith!" (Hebrews 11)

CONTENTS

FOREWORD

Five years ago I spoke at a conference in Canada where two-thirds of the attendees were Canadian missionaries and the remaining one-third were First Nations people. The conference theme was "Partnership." After opening remarks, I asked the group a question: "What comes to your mind when you hear the word *partnership*?" The missionary members offered words like *mutuality, sharing, respect, cooperation, collaboration* and so on. It struck me that, as far as I could tell, none of the First Nations people had spoken. After a long silence, a First Nations person spoke firmly but dispassionately: "When we hear the word *partnership*, what comes to our mind is that this is another way for the White man to control us."

In my forty years of experience on the international scene, I have heard similar expressions echoed in many other parts of the world. For this reason and others, Mary Lederleitner's book will find enthusiastic acclaim by global peoples who want to follow Christ in greater unity and with greater effectiveness.

The reader will be impressed with four important thoughts. First, the book addresses fairly and thoroughly the tough, thorny financial issues in cross-cultural partnerships. Second, the book provides reasoned, sound biblical interpretation that directs us toward healthy solutions. Third, the perspectives in this book are sensitive to and respectful of cultural realities and therefore more likely to sustain strong partnerships. Finally, this book provides principles that are transferable across cultures. Mary's expansive experiences and depth of understanding qualifies her to take us to new places where we can see things more clearly and act more responsibly, the end result being wiser stewardship while building the global body of Christ.

With surgical skill, Mary has exposed the wounds and toxins that have infected missionary–host people relations for decades. With a gentle spirit she repeatedly shows where good intentions have been undermined by defective cultural understanding and by hidden assumptions such as the prevalent, but usually unconscious, "My way is the better way." Her verbal scalpel cuts deeply into our past practices but without inducing guilt in the readers. Who of us has not made mistakes? She humbly admits her own failures while suggesting better ways, healing ways, based on sound biblical reflection and careful cultural exegesis. Her ease in admitting and learning from her own mistakes allows us to do the same and find new possibilities for redemptive partnerships.

The chapter on Scripture and accountability opens wonderful insights necessary for a sound foundation. The section on core cultural concepts, while drawing on historically accepted ideas, launches us into refreshing new ways of application for those of us looking for contextualization of partnership.

In my opinion, most central to the book is the chapter on dignity and mutuality. A shared commitment to honoring each other's dignity establishes the prerequisite for any hope of mutuality. Unfortunately, human dignity, while much discussed in recent years, remains elusive in practice. But if brothers and sisters in the global church can keep human dignity at the front of our conversation, we will manage to accomplish two things: it will keep us grounded in the centrality of the image of God who created and loves each person, and it will then follow that we must commit never to dehumanize one whom God has confirmed with his image. To paraphrase C. S. Lewis, every human encounter is intended to be a sacred moment by honoring the dignity of the other person; anything less is to deform the image of God in that person and thus profane the moment and the God who created them (Proverbs 14:31; Matthew 25:40).

Whereas many have criticized missionaries and missionary practices without offering adequate alternatives, Mary generously affirms so much that is done right. More importantly, the help she offers is not only empowering but restorative for the soul of the missionary and, yes, also for the host country person who benefits from mutual understanding. At this point her book stands as a model for others who would seek to help the global mission of the church. In summary, it would be hard to overestimate the value of this book for sound wisdom in building and sustaining international partnerships.

Duane H. Elmer, Ph.D.
G. W. Aldeen Professor of International Studies and Mission
Distinguished Professor of Educational Studies, Ph.D. Program
Trinity International University/Trinity Evangelical Divinity School

PREFACE

Interspersed throughout this book are many personal stories. In each, the details have been modified to ensure confidentiality. Great care has been taken to protect the identities of those who have been willing to share their experiences with me over the past decade. In many instances, different leaders working in diverse settings around the world have told the same plotlines to me on numerous occasions. Because of this, any similarities to specific names and instances you might know about are purely coincidental.

I wish it were possible to provide you with a truly "global" perspective in the purest sense of that term. I wish I could share thoughts and ideas without any bias and without ever reflecting my own culture of origin. As I grow older, however, I increasingly realize that I need to be honest about who I am. I cannot give a fully global perspective because I live within the skin and body of a person born, raised and educated in the United States. This is both a blessing and a hindrance at times.

I have tried to carefully and thoughtfully capture the ideas and frustrations of friends and mission leaders from other cultures in this text. Despite the care taken to do this well, I am sure it still falls short. For that I truly apologize. Nonetheless, since I am from the United States, I am able to speak candidly and directly about the common blind spots and weaknesses of those who share my cultural heritage. Some of the keenest insights I have learned about cross-cultural partnership have come out of my own mistakes. I am far from perfect, and I still have much to learn when it comes to partnering well across cultures. In that sense, I hope this book will bring healing and a sense that we are "in this together." My deep hope and prayer is that it will foster heartfelt and creative dialogue that will take us to a better place in global missions.

ACKNOWLEDGMENTS

While writing this book, my mind often drifted to two things. Only by the grace of God will I ever be able to make a meaningful contribution to the mission community. That truth I know in the deepest core of my being. The second truth coincides with the working out of that grace. Over the years, God has enabled me to cross paths with many truly extraordinary people who took time from their busy schedules to build into my character or to extend unique and exciting ministry opportunities. I would now like to thank these people. Each helped to shape how I think and how I see the world, which in turn has significantly influenced this manuscript.

I would especially like to thank my parents, John and Marty Mallon. I love them and miss them greatly. They were always willing to welcome new people into their lives. I think this "way of being" is at the heart of any effective outreach or mission program. I also thank all my siblings, especially my brother Tom and his wife, Margaret Mary, who have been such significant influences in my life and ministry. And I thank my incredible husband, John Lederleitner, who always encourages me and never laughs when I come up with crazy ideas like writing a book!

I thank Carol Nichols, Jay Halley and Terry Bowman, who were such great mentors for me when I was a young believer. I thank Alice Petersen who gave me my first opportunity to work on a church staff. I learned so much from her and others at College Hill Presbyterian Church. I also thank Andy Morgan who hired me to serve in the singles ministry at Christ Church of Oak Brook. Together we focused on a ministry of lay empowerment, and to this day it remains as one of my most joyful memories. I have also learned a great deal from Doug and Adele Calhoun, who have been incredible pastors for me over the years.

In addition to these mentors, my thinking has been enhanced and enriched by many excellent professors at Wheaton College and Trinity Evangelical Divinity School. All of my professors have been extraordinary, but I would especially like to thank Scott Moreau, Evvy Campbell and Duane Elmer, who have been great mentors and friends.

From my Wycliffe life I would like to thank Dave Cram. He often took risks and entrusted me with unique and significant ministry roles. Because of this I have been able to travel to many countries around the world, work with all kinds of diverse ministries, and still have the opportunity to do research as well. Had he not given me these opportunities, I would not have the practical experience to write a book like this. Friends who have prayed and financially supported me over the years with Wycliffe have been equally important for without them I could have never stepped into any of these positions.

Many others have helped in the editing and publishing of this manuscript. John Jusu's keen insights about cross-cultural partnerships have been invaluable. Don Fiddler, a retired high school English teacher from Faith Academy, has been an enormous blessing. My editor, Al Hsu, has been a great encouragement as well.

Last but not least are the countless missionaries and indigenous leaders who have inspired me more than they will ever know. They are utterly amazing. Their commitment to missions, their sacrificial living, and their willingness to put their lives on the line so others might "just have a chance" to accept Jesus as their Lord and Savior have left a deep and lasting impact on my life. All of this they do without any promise or certainty of success. They are my modern-day heroes of faith. Whether expatriate staff or national colleagues, they inspire me to the depths of my being! My deep hope is that this book will have ripple effects that will make their work a bit easier.

INTRODUCTION

PARTNERSHIP, MONEY
AND CULTURAL INTELLIGENCE

Cross-cultural partnerships are on the rise.[1] They have become a primary method in which churches and organizations engage in global missions.[2] Partners from different cultures and contexts start working together with the hope of accomplishing great things for the kingdom of God. Yet despite their noble dreams and aspirations, working through cultural differences that surround money can become overwhelming at times. Over the years I have witnessed often that these cultural differences about how funds are utilized and accounted for cause cross-cultural partnerships to come unglued.[3] When this happens, many relationships are ruptured and the witness of Christ is hindered (see John 17:20-21).

For this reason I believe it is very important to carefully study issues related to culture and money, so we can work more effectively with cross-cultural partners. We need to grow in cultural intelligence, so we are a blessing and not a hindrance to God's purposes in the world. The following true story is one of many examples that illustrates this need for greater awareness and understanding. I wish I could say that it is unusual because the outcome is a sad one. However, the things that happen in this story are common. I have heard similar stories in many different parts of the world.

THE "SISTER CHURCH" PARTNERSHIP

I knew Mark had seen a lot of interesting partnership situations over the years as he served as a liaison for church-planting ministries in Eastern Europe.[4] As we talked over lunch he told me a story that still haunts me to this day. Despite truly good intentions, things can go terribly wrong.

Alex was born and raised in a country in Eastern Europe that had come out from under communism in the late 1980s. Although Christianity had for the most part been banned under the prior regime, there was now newfound freedom to share Christ and start churches. God blessed Alex's outreach efforts, and through his ministry a church was planted. The congregation exceeded two hundred committed believers and exhibited a vibrant and growing faith. People were maturing in Christ and church members had great love for one another. It was also a giving congregation. They always helped one another as needs arose, and they often gave sacrificially to the many fruitful ministries being spawned by members in the congregation.

In its initial stage the congregation met in an old theater. During this time a church in the United States learned about this congregation. Through mutual acquaintances, the American church decided to visit and learn more about what was happening in this exciting ministry. Their mission pastor visited, and over time the American church felt they should adopt the Eastern European congregation as a "sister church." This special relationship would enable them to work more closely together, send short-term mission teams to the area, and invest in a part of the world that had not had a strong Christian presence for a long time. The Eastern European congregation liked having American "brothers and sisters." It would enable them to share in each other's lives and to see Christ's work advance even more quickly. So the special relationship was formed and both parties had high hopes for how things would develop in the future.

The American church explained it was making a ten-year commitment to help the congregation in Eastern Europe. Both sides understood that this was the promise of the American church. As a whole it was a good relationship, and both partners were blessed because of it. However, during the seventh year, things changed. Ed, the senior pastor of the American church, came to visit the sister church. His intent was to deepen the bonds between the two churches and better understand the struggles their Eastern European brothers and sisters were facing. The Eastern European church was coming through a very difficult stretch. They always paid their rent on time, but for reasons beyond their control, they needed to keep moving their services to different locations. The owner of the movie theater where they rented space decided to demolish the building. The church then rented storefronts, but the owners of the properties converted those into high-end retail space. This happened several times. The Eastern European church then rented space in a school. However, after a year or so a new law was passed in the country saying that no government property could be rented for any reason to any religious organization. Despite all of their faithfulness, they were continually being evicted, and fewer and fewer viable options remained.

Each time the church had to change locations they lost people, for in addition to the many committed believers there were many seekers too. The differing sites meant meeting in diverse and distant parts of the city, and many who were just learning about

Christ for the first time were unwilling to make the additional commute. At times the church was literally homeless, setting up tents and meeting in parks during winter months when temperatures were well below freezing. Despite the regular loss of new visitors and seekers, the church still had over two hundred members who continued to come amidst all the turmoil and hardships. Church members continued to give to the ministry. However, their tithes and offerings were not enough to buy land and build a sanctuary as the average church member earned only approximately $250 per month. Although members tithed and gave sacrificially, their personal resources were insufficient to buy a building that would cost in excess of $75,000 while still supporting a pastor and the others ministries of the church. In addition, in this country banks would not extend a long-term mortgage to religious organizations.

When Alex explained this pressing need, Ed explained that he would do "everything within his power" to help. Alex explained that a viable option would be to build a church building on his property behind his house. The land would be donated, and the sanctuary could be built for approximately $50,000, well below the cost of purchasing a building somewhere else. Ed asked for a business plan, and the church did careful research and provided one. Ed also asked for a copy of the blueprints, so Alex worked with an architect to provide this as well. During the visit, Ed took all kinds of detailed measurements and pictures. He also explained that his church in America was in the midst of a building project and it was likely they could tithe what they received to cover the cost of this new building for their sister church.

Ed went home, and everyone in the Eastern European church was convinced that the funding would come for the new facility. Members of the Eastern European church went online frequently at a local Internet café so they already knew their sister church was in the midst of a $6,000,000 building campaign, not for a new sanctuary but simply to expand their vestibule and add a coffee bar. Surely, $50,000 was not too much to share with their "sister," was it? It was less than 1 percent of the funding they were raising to cover what already looked to them to be an incredibly beautiful facility.

Ed returned to the United States and the Eastern European church waited for a response. In the interim, the Eastern European church again lost their rented property through absolutely no fault of their own. They were again homeless and meeting in a park with winter fast approaching. Knowing that Ed promised to do everything in his power to make this happen, they began borrowing from everyone in the community to start building a sanctuary behind Alex's home. Members in the church gave even more sacrificially, and among themselves they raised 10 percent of the funds outright by selling things they owned and depleting their savings accounts. However, they borrowed the remaining $45,000 from local businesses, relatives and even non-Christian neighbors. To every creditor they explained what Ed had said during his visit and what he did, taking specific measurements and photos, and all understood that to mean the funds would surely be coming soon from America to reimburse everyone.

The new church in Eastern Europe was built, but for some reason Ed was not communicating. He was neither returning calls nor answering emails. That is when my friend Mark was contacted by the church in Eastern Europe to follow up and understand why their sister church in America was delaying the funds and no longer communicating. Mark tried to contact the senior pastor and for about six months there was no response. Finally, Ed returned Mark's calls and sheepishly confessed that he could not "sell" his congregation on the idea of funding this new church building in Eastern Europe. Ed said he just took up an offering and would be sending what he was able to raise, which was only $4,000. The

American church's building program was not going well and was
behind schedule. So Ed's leadership team felt they should not be
sending funds abroad until they met their own target at home.
Mark was faced with the unbelievably unpleasant task of sharing
this news with the sister church.

Mark said it was horrible. Alex was incensed. Mark did some
research to try to find out why the Eastern Europeans were convinced that a promise had been made when Ed thought he had
only communicated that he would "try." Part of the misunderstanding came from a translation incident and the meaning of the
phrase of speech used. When Mark asked another Eastern European from the region who was not part of the congregation what
the phrase meant, he was told it was a binding promise. There is a
phrase that is very similar but is not a binding promise. However,
Mark said it is likely that the translator communicated the binding phrase as she knew how much Alex wanted and needed the
building, and she wanted to facilitate a good relationship between
the two men during the visit. The outside advisor working with
Mark also said that even if a different phrase of speech had been
used, any confusion or ambiguity would have been alleviated
when Ed followed up by acquiring detailed specs and pictures of
the property, and requiring such a detailed business plan. Even if
the words were confusing, the actions of the senior pastor were
crystal clear. In that culture it was obvious that the American
church had the capacity, willingness and commitment as a sister
church to help. Otherwise, why would the senior pastor waste
everyone's time with so many complicated questions?

Mark said the whole thing made him want to cry. He contacted
a number of missionaries in the region and explained the story.
The missionaries raised $15,000 among themselves for the church.
However, this still left an enormous shortfall. The Eastern European church lost standing with businessmen and unbelievers in

the community as they were unable to pay their debt in a timely way. The church lost a lot of members, but those who are still there are faithfully trying to pay off the debt. With such small salaries, they will be paying on it for decades.

The saddest part of the story though was what happened to Alex. Mark said he became quite bitter because in his context in a former communist country, the greatest sin of all is hoarding and not sharing with others. He felt the American church was sinful to spend so much money to expand a vestibule and add a coffee bar, all the while not caring that their "sister" did not even have a roof over her head. Alex felt any kind of Christianity that promoted such behavior could not be genuine. If that was what having a "sister" was like, they were better off without one. The seven-year relationship came to an abrupt end, and Mark said it is taking Alex years to work through the bitterness and anger in his soul.

LEARNING FROM OUR MISTAKES

The beautiful thing about cultural intelligence[5] is that, if we are willing to keep learning, we never have to be defined by our past mistakes.[6] Every situation, even those where we fail, can foster deep learning that will enable us to be a true blessing in the future. I believe *in Christ* it is possible to see better outcomes in ministry. Instead of attacking one another when we encounter different views about how to spend or account for resources, we can choose to slow down and consider the bigger picture. We can develop genuine respect for the different ways in which we work. We can take stock of lessons learned by others and begin to develop better ways of working together. We can navigate conflict in ways that will strengthen rather than destroy our relationships.

Appendix A provides a tool to help you apply what you learn from this case study to your own ministry context. While I will

share positive stories about cross-cultural partnerships later, I
hope this story creates a sense of urgency. Good intentions are not
enough to ensure good outcomes in cross-cultural partnerships.
We need to be willing to keep learning to be fruitful in missions.
Thankfully, we serve a redemptive God who can take the heartache of this type of story and use it as a springboard for great good
in the future.

BRIEF OVERVIEW

In the following chapters we will uncover a multitude of issues
that intersect with the topics of money, mission and culture. We
will examine core cultural concepts that explain why people hold
diverse beliefs about financial resources. We will look at premature judgments and the potency of the "meaning-making" process. We will explore paternalism and the role it plays in the accountability process. We will look at common unintended
consequences experienced by those who partner in diverse contexts around the world. We will examine the complexities of the
financial dependency debate and begin to understand why a "one
size fits all" answer is often inappropriate given the diversity present in the global mission context.

We will look at passages of Scripture that will enable us to view
financial accountability with a fresh perspective. We will learn
why it is so important to critically contextualize accountability
processes. We will look at ways we can foster dignity and mutuality in our cross-cultural relationships. We will also look at how to
build capacity and sustainability in our mission efforts.

Since conflict is inevitable when we work closely in cross-
cultural partnerships, we will also look at a number of diverse
conflict-resolution strategies that foster better outcomes. We will
explore what to do when funds are not used for designated pur-

poses or when fraud or theft occurs. We will unpack a passage of Scripture rich in encouragement and exhortation for those seeking to do cross-cultural partnerships well. Finally, the epilogue offers two stories showing why cross-cultural partners need one another to mature and grow into the full nature of Christ Jesus.

You will find additional practical help in the appendices as well. Appendix A provides a tool for you to use the above case study to gain insights that will help your ministry. Appendix B has questions that can foster deeper dialogue as leaders seek to develop a culture of fiscal integrity within a ministry or cross-cultural partnership. Appendix C provides a recommended reading list for those who would like to delve more deeply into these various issues. As we begin to understand these concepts, we will be able to better navigate the complexities of money and mission. Let's get started!

Part One

CORE CULTURAL
CONCEPTS

Is It "Mine" or "Ours"?

At the level of symbols one also finds money. Money has no intrinsic
value, nor an intrinsic meaning, other than that which is attributed to it
by convention. It also means different things to different people.

—Geert Hofstede and Gert Jan Hofstede

As I work with people involved in cross-cultural partnership, I
have often heard North Americans say things like, "Well, you
know—they are into that collective thing! They do not care about
financial accountability and integrity!" Majority World leaders
have expressed at times their own sentiments to me, "Well, you
know, those Americans are totally obsessed with money! That is
all that matters to them! They just don't care about people!" What
amazes me as I hear these comments is each time, the person
making such statements believes he or she totally understands the
cultural issues involved. Time and again the person making the
comments believes he or she is the seasoned cross-cultural worker.
Yet as the words roll off their lips, I realize they still do not genuinely understand. How can I make such a claim? I can tell because
their comments are not seasoned with respect.

Paul Hiebert was a deeply respected missiologist whose writings have had a significant impact on many engaged in missions. He wrote that people tend to think "their culture is civilized and that others are primitive and backward."[1] Few of us realize how ethnocentric we really are. It is only when we encounter people with different beliefs and attitudes that we realize how intensely we hold certain views. Hiebert writes, "We often see the basic assumptions underlying another culture better than we recognize our own. . . . Similarly, foreigners often see our assumptions more clearly than we do, and we need to listen to what they say about us. Our initial reaction is often to reject their observations as overly critical. On further reflection, however, we often find them to be true."[2]

In order to work together well we need to listen to one another. We need to not only deeply grasp how our partners feel and what they believe but also take the additional step to understand why such feelings and beliefs are wholly logical within a given context. If we can see the logic of a person's worldview, if we can value it as being wholly reasonable given a unique cultural heritage and history, from that place of mutual respect and dignity we can find new and creative ways to overcome obstacles and work together. If we never take that step, at some level within our hearts we will continue to demean how others think and function in the world. When it comes to money and cross-cultural ministry partnerships, a misunderstanding of individualistic and collectivistic worldviews is often at the heart of our most destructive ministry conflicts.

WHAT DO THE TERMS MEAN?

It is impossible to talk about any one nation or culture and say that everyone within it functions exactly the same way. To make such an assertion would be too simplistic. However, with regard to money and worldviews, there is a spectrum. People tend to fall either more on the side of individualism or collectivism as they interact with people and the world around them. If partners are coming from one worldview and they begin working with partners functioning from another place on that continuum, it can cause a great deal of conflict and confusion.

Understanding individualism. Geert Hofstede is an organizational anthropologist who has spent much of his life studying how culture affects people's ability to work together. Years later his son Gert joined him in this research. They found that in individualistic cultures "everyone is expected to look after himself or herself and his or her immediate family."[3] Children "learn to think of themselves as 'I' and neither practically nor psychologically is the healthy person in this type of society supposed to be dependent on a group."[4] Money is one of the ways people define maturity and success in individualistic cultures. If a person "manages money well," he or she is deemed to be wise. Within a church or Christian setting, such a person is seen as being a "good steward" of God's resources. As such, he or she is often granted more responsibility and authority. For instance, in the United States it is common for people like this to be elected as elders or trustees of churches and ministries. If a person acquires a lot of money in the broader secular culture, he or she is often admired by others since that wealth will likely ensure even greater autonomy and security from hardships.

Understanding collectivism. The problem that arises is that researchers have uncovered that the "vast majority of the world lives in societies in which the interests of the group prevail over the interests of the individual. We will call these societies collectivistic."[5] Of these cultures the Hofstedes write,

> Personal opinions do not exist—they are predetermined by
> the group. . . . A child who repeatedly voices opinions deviat-

ing from what is collectively felt is considered to have a bad character. . . . The loyalty to the group that is an essential element of the collectivist family also means that resources are shared. If one member of an extended family of twenty persons has a paid job and the others do not, the earning member is supposed to share his or her income in order to help feed the entire family. On the basis of this principle, a family may collectively cover the expenses for sending one member to get a higher education, expecting that when this member subsequently gets a well-paid job, the income will also be shared.[6]

Researchers have shown that "members of collectivistic cultures learn different major values (e.g., harmony, solidarity) and acquire different preferred ways to conceive of themselves (e.g., as interconnected with others)."[7] In this worldview it is understood that putting the group first is the way to ensure security from future hardships. A person who is saving resources when others around are in need is viewed as being a bad Christian.

How does it work? Sometimes we do not grasp how implicitly and deeply these distinct values have been ingrained in us. It starts from the time we are babies and toddlers. In the United States it is common that one of the first words a child learns to speak is *mine!* A Korean friend of mine explained the implicit nature of collectivism. In the Korean language there are no individual possessive pronouns. She explained that if her mother came from another region to visit her in college, my friend would introduce her to everyone as "our mother." If entire languages do not even acknowledge individual possession, is it any wonder that cross-cultural partners frequently view financial resources differently?

Why Did These Distinct Worldviews Develop?

In the book *African Friends and Money Matters,*[8] David Maranz illustrates the validity of the two different worldviews. He explains that the most important consideration in African economies is "the distribution of economic resources so that all persons may have their minimum needs met, or at least that they may survive."[9] While he was writing the book, the employment rate in Dakar, Senegal, at the time was about 30 percent. That meant that approximately 70 percent of the adults living in the capital of that country did not have a full-time job. He wrote that "in the midst of these seemingly permanently impossible conditions people continue to eat, are clothed and housed, and they survive. Those who have even meager means share with kin and close friends. There are no riots. People live their lives with, it seems to me, at least as much contentment as Westerners do in their home countries. Of course, they all hope for better days, but in the meantime, they make the most of their situations."[10]

Maranz explains that the unemployment rate in France at that same time was 11 percent and this was a catalyst for riots and all kinds of unhappiness. During the Great Depression in the United States, the unemployment rate was only 25 percent, and it seemed as though the entire country was going to collapse. For these reasons, it is helpful to see that the collectivistic way of viewing money does foster good outcomes in many situations.

Maranz explains that the primary economic consideration in individualistic cultures is "the accumulation of capital and wealth. . . . The average Westerner lives, in many material ways at least, better than most kings of the past."[11] This accumulation of personal wealth has enabled many Christians to donate large sums of money to fund cross-cultural partnerships. In many individualistic cultures, the higher standard of living means that there is often an extensive infrastructure and all kinds of support mechanisms in place. For this reason, people can "cultivate friends solely for emotional ends. They separate emotional needs from economic needs

as the two are met in such different ways."[12] Money and wealth, not
relationships, form the foundation for personal security.

Maranz's insights can keep partners from individualistic cultures from feeling smug or superior. We are able to separate money
from friendships only because we have an infrastructure that per-
mits such a thing. It is not the way the world has normally oper-
ated. If we realize this, we are more able to face the differing expectations with grace and kindness.

Even in my own life I see the power of infrastructure on individualistic and collective behaviors. I live on a little street with
about ten other families. We get together once a year for a block
party. We talk occasionally as we cut our grass or work in the
yard. However, most of the time we go about our own individual
lives not very aware how each person is doing or what struggles
they are facing. All of this can change in an instant though.

As soon as there is a blackout, we all start going outside. We begin asking, "Do you have electricity? Do you have water? Is your
basement flooding?" We transition quite quickly from incredibly
independent neighbors to a little collective community that carefully watches out for one another. We share snow blowers or gen-
erators or whatever else someone might need. But as soon as the
power comes back on, we go back to our independent lives. Individualism is a luxury that can only be maintained if there is a
healthy, growing economy and a well-developed national infrastructure. Since many people take those things for granted, we misunderstand others who approach life without those safety nets.

WHAT DOES THE BIBLE SAY ABOUT THESE WORLDVIEWS?

What is fascinating to me is how we can find support for both
worldviews in Scripture. When it comes to personal accountability and individualism, there are parables that teach these themes.

Jesus explains the story of the ten virgins in Matthew 25:1-13 and the parable of the talents in Matthew 25:14-30. Amidst the plot lines, individuals were held accountable for specific resources, and they were rewarded or disciplined depending on the results achieved. Scripture also provides teaching about saving and leaving an inheritance in Proverbs 13:22. With regard to a collectivistic worldview, we see passages supporting that way of thinking as well. In Matthew 6:19-34 Jesus tells us not to lay aside treasures in this life as an effort to protect ourselves in the future. Second Corinthians 8:13-14 and Acts 2:41-47 indicate that we should share so all believers have their basic needs met. We see this same theme in James 2:14-17.

Perhaps the most stunning aspect is how God admonishes people in both worldviews. As I have reflected deeply on both perspectives, it appears to me that each way of viewing life has an innate bent toward sin. To the individualist Christ admonishes us in Matthew 6:24 that we must love God more than money. To the collectivists Jesus says in Matthew 10:37 that if we do not love him more than our family members, we are not worthy of him. What does this mean? I think it indicates that we all need to keep growing and maturing. Perhaps the answer is not an either-or philosophy that applies across the board but rather something that needs to be assessed in each unique situation. Neither worldview causes us to be immune from making idols out of things in our cultures that foster a sense of security.

IMPLICATIONS FOR CROSS-CULTURAL PARTNERSHIPS

How do these different worldviews interact when we come together to form cross-cultural partnerships? What are key areas most prone to tension? How do these two differing dimensions of culture create misunderstandings?

How we "do" partnership. In a presentation about cross-cultural ministry partnerships, John Watters from Wycliffe International outlined two key areas where there is a common disconnect. He said, "Africans define partnership as a long-term relationship, extending even beyond one's death. Metaphors like *marriage*, and *older brother–younger brother* are used to describe the relationship. The first order of business is "courting," getting to know one another, assessing whether or not the relationship holds promise. Expatriates define partnership as a business contract for a specified time period—and the first order of business is writing up a memorandum of understanding."[13]

In more individualistic cultures we tend to confuse our nomenclature. We do things like form "partnerships" with "sister churches." We like the family nomenclature. It makes us feel warm and connected. Then in the next breath we will draw up our ten- or fifteen-year partnership agreement or memorandum of understanding to outline the relationship and confirm that at the end of a certain period there will no longer be any financial support. Those from individualistic cultures rarely sense the disconnect, yet the term *family* is supposed to mean forever. So we need to be careful not to confuse our partners with language that says one thing and actions that indicate another.

Loans function differently. I had a friend who was managing an office overseas, and one of his cross-cultural ministry partners, who had taken out a loan a few years earlier, finally paid it off in its entirety. That partner never missed nor was he ever late with a single financial payment. My friend said he was so glad that his partner was now out from under the debt. Two weeks later this same person approached him to take out a much larger loan.

My friend, trying to persuade him in Christian love, began sharing Scriptures with him to explain why he should not be living in debt. The national partner looked extremely annoyed, and thankfully my friend picked up on this and asked for his partner's perspective on the situation. His national partner said something that has always stuck with me. He said, "I am borrowing a large sum of money from you to show that I am committed to being your partner for many years to come and to show that I respect you. If my debt is paid off, it means I can leave this partnership at any time. There is no obligation any more and therefore no commitment. I am asking for this loan to show you how committed I am to this ministry." I asked my friend, "So what did you do?" He said, "Well, initially I sat there for a few moments, feeling like a total idiot. Then I gave him the loan!"

Loans do not always function the same way abroad. I know of another instance where two partnering organizations took extensive care to draw up loan agreements and repayment schedules so the Majority World partner could purchase a much-needed asset for the ministry. However, when the partner delayed in making payments, the Western partner got upset. The Majority World partner did not understand the problem. The issue was not that either side had been deceitful or dishonest. Instead, the two organizations used "family" nomenclature. And in that culture family members did draw up loan agreements when relatives borrowed money. However, everyone there knows that if a less affluent family member delays paying back a loan to a wealthier family member, the wealthier person will be patient and understand. He or she would never confront or put pressure on the poorer family member, for to do so would cause shame and create disharmony in the relationship. The wealthier person has sufficient means and will not be hurt by the delayed payments.

Both of these cross-cultural ministry partners thought they had communicated before transacting a loan. However, neither stepped back to see the cultural expectations they were carrying into the agreement. These were "implicit" to each, despite truly good intentions and extensive cross-cultural experience.

Gifts are very tricky. In individualistic cultures, if things are given out of obligation, we feel they have less merit or value. Such gifts seem insincere to us. This goes back to the principles Maranz described in that we like to separate financial obligations from true friendships.

Gifts in collective cultures work quite differently though. Often gift giving is a step taken to create future obligations, thus tying people together in what are often invisible yet very real bonds. Large gifts come with large expectations. Accepting a gift that does not seem large to the receiving partner but is perceived as being large to the giving partner will often convey a willingness to help the less affluent partner in the future. For this reason, it is important to consult with people who know the culture well. Otherwise, you might be conveying a very different message or you might be entering into informal contractual obligations without even realizing it.

Stealing is often defined differently. In many individualistic cultures stealing is defined as taking a possession that belongs to another person and using it for our own personal benefit without the owner's prior consent or permission. In many cultural contexts, any resource already belongs to the entire community. If it is not being used by the current owner, it is allowed to be borrowed and used by others at any time. This creates a lot of confusion when it comes to financial resources and donor designated funds. For this reason, it is important to look at this issue carefully with leaders before entering into partnerships. We will cover this in greater detail throughout book. The thing to remember at this point is that because of this dynamic, many Christian leaders might not feel they are stealing anything. In fact, for many, not sharing resources is deemed to be a far greater sin before God.

INDIRECT IMPLICATIONS

There are many direct implications to these diverse worldviews when it comes to the intersection of mission, money and culture. However, as we begin interacting with partners in other cultures, these worldviews spawn a number of indirect issues as well. We will begin to address these in the next chapter.

COMMUNICATION AND HARMONY

Sometimes American partners are tolerated, in some cases respected, and at other times admired. But in this instance Art had superseded all these categorizations. His partners genuinely and deeply loved him. He had worked overseas for many years, and there was a warmth and authenticity in his relationships with others that drew people toward him. He was never condescending. It was obvious that love and deep mutual respect went both ways.

Yet with all his international experience, Art had not fully grasped the impact that status played in group decision making. Art believed he had a great idea for a way to train young Christian leaders from the region. He had done a lot of research and when the group came together from many countries, he presented the idea and took a vote. He was ecstatic at the response. All of the cross-cultural partners voted unanimously in favor of his proposal. Art left the meetings thrilled at the progress that was made and the level of unity within the group. It was not until months later, when the cross-cultural partners never submitted their portion of the funds needed to make it happen, that he started to be confused and frustrated. In his mind he thought, *We talked about it. The full plan was presented. They all voted in favor of it. Why are they not honoring their word and sending in the funds pledged in that decision?*

Later another colleague began meeting one-on-one with many of these leaders. In those informal discussions it became obvious that these partners never agreed with the plan. They felt they had no time to discuss it or consider any other options. Instead, a vote was forced. Because they wholly loved Art, they did not want to dishonor or cause him to lose face with a dissenting vote. They felt to do so would deeply shame him and his role as a leader. So they all voted yes but answered no by their actions. The plan fell apart, and many were hurt in the process.

UNDERSTANDING "FACE"

A core concept in many collective societies is "face." Many people in individualistic cultures make the mistake of assuming it is the same thing as reputation. However, its meaning and role in society is far greater. Individualistic cultures navigate life by utilizing a currency of money, but collectivistic cultures navigate life by using a currency of face.

Intercultural researchers explain that it "is a symbolic resource in social interaction because this resource can be threatened, enhanced, maintained, and bargained over."[1] An Asian sociologist once wrote, "While it is not a necessity for one to strive to gain face, losing face is a serious matter which will, in varying degrees, affect one's ability to function effectively in society. Face is lost when the individual, either through his action or that of people closely related to him, fails to meet essential requirements placed upon him by virtue of the social position he occupies."[2] The best comparison I have found to explain the seriousness of the concept of "losing face" is to compare it to a person in an individualistic culture who has just discovered that a criminal has stolen his or her entire pension fund. In much the same way, both individuals will now have a very hard time finding any measure of security within their perspective societies. The resource they needed to navigate their cultures—money in one instance and face in the other—has been seriously eroded.

It is interesting in this story that face was gravely affecting the meeting and process even though Art was not concerned about protecting his own face. Art was a gregarious and fun-loving soul who never took himself too seriously. Yet because his partners were Asians, they were deeply concerned about how they treated him in a public forum. It was their love and care for him that caused them to act in ways that would, from their own cultural perspective, protect his face.

Understanding status. A concept closely tied to face is status. In some cultures the emphasis is on status that is achieved. For instance, if someone graduates top of their class, starts a successful business or gets drafted by a major league sports franchise, the person usually enjoys high status within the community. In other cultures, status might be ascribed based on skin color, birthright, gender or other criteria. In many cultures status plays a critical role in communication.

Some cultures have what is called "low power distance," which means it is largely egalitarian, and status among people is minimized. It is easy to approach people and speak directly even about contentious issues. Other cultures function from "high power distance." People in these cultures accept that power is not shared. There is a great deal of distance between those with power and those without power. Yet those with power are expected to care for those under them. These cultures often have specific ways and protocols in which sensitive issues or concerns can be presented and considered to those holding power.[3]

Another ironic feature in the story about Art is he was not concerned about status. He was very egalitarian by nature. He treated everyone with kindness and respect. He did not feel his position should ever be used to coerce or manipulate anyone. Quite the contrary. He wanted to truly know what people were thinking and feeling. However, whether he liked it or not, his partners were from cultures that deeply valued status issues. Since Art had such a high status in his organization, they were not going to behave in any way in a public setting that would disrespect or dishonor the status that he possessed.

High and low context cultures. In addition to face and status, there is a third concept that influences communication. Some cultures are low context, which means they rely heavily on words, both written and spoken, to discern meaning. These are often cultures that are comfortable with more direct methods of communication. They are also often those with a more individualistic and egalitarian worldview. Many others are quite different. High context cultures place very little stock in words. They often do not believe what people say. Instead, they look to the context or actions to determine meaning.[4] In these cultures there is often little concern if words do not match actions. High context communication often evolve in contexts where there is high power distance and people are simply unable to say no or give unwelcome advice or input for fear of causing another to lose face. In other scenarios the power differential might be so great that people cannot speak directly for fear of losing their lives. In these situations, the method of communication might linger long after a repressive regime has been removed.

We see this dynamic at play in Art's situation. Art presented the idea first in a public forum. He had not allowed time to process the ideas in what would be considered a safe and nonthreatening environment. His Asian partners would always process things one-on-one or in informal settings before arranging for a

public discussion or forum. They voted yes with their words but
no by their actions.

HOW SHOULD CROSS-CULTURAL PARTNERS RESPOND?

If we are not careful, we can harbor prejudice against the form of
communication and status used or valued in a different culture.
People working in cross-cultural ministry tend to respond in one
of three ways.

We can ignore issues of status. Duane Elmer explains the outcome of this choice as he tells a story from his early years as a
missionary in Africa. He was the head of a Bible school. The grass
around the school was getting long and he thought he would
model servanthood to the students by rolling up his sleeves and
cutting the grounds late one Friday afternoon.[5] He explained that
he felt somewhat proud of himself for being the type of leader that
was humble and willing to do any job. He thought the students
would be touched and impressed by his actions. When Monday
rolled around and the students arrived, they were deeply upset
because Duane's actions had dishonored him and the institution.
When people in the community saw Duane mowing the grounds,
they interpreted it to mean that he was a poor manager, unable to
oversee even the grounds personnel and that the school must not
be run very well. How did they come to such a conclusion? Duane
was a white missionary leading a Bible school and he had numerous graduate degrees. For such a high-status person to do such a
low-status job like mowing the lawn brought dishonor to him and
the institution he served.

Whenever I think of that story, I am grateful that Duane was
willing to share it. I am also overwhelmed at how, amidst our best
intentions, we can innocently do things that hinder ministry and
the advancement of the gospel. His story illustrates what can hap-

pen when we remain uninformed regarding the issues of status within a culture.

We can impose our views on others. Judith Lingenfelter illustrates this option. She writes,

> The culture of prestige often surprises foreign teachers. In some places in Asia, students stand and either bow or clap when the teacher enters the classroom. Some western teachers comment on how uncomfortable this makes them feel, and one person told me that she vigorously discouraged this practice in her classes. What she did not realize was that she was breaking down respect patterns concerning the ascribed status of a teacher. The consequences of such a seemingly innocuous decision may not surface until many years later.[6]

This is common in university settings in North America too. Many well-meaning professors can "insist" that students refer to them by their first names. However, many students arriving from overseas are horribly uncomfortable addressing the professor without the appropriate title of Dr. It is one thing to encourage warmth; however, we do not want to impose it on others. If we are in our own context, the better option is to tell people a variety of ways in which they can address us, and let them pick the one that puts *them* most at ease. If we are in another culture, we need to be exceedingly careful to not change customs unless we wholly understand all the implications. We should seek change only if wise counselors from inside the culture push in favor of the change as well. Otherwise, rather than helping people, we may be making life more difficult for them.

We can respect status issues and work within them. This is my preference, especially when it comes to the area of financial accountability in cultures. I have seen some mission agencies navigate this well. For instance, if a partner is a high-status person in the culture who needs to be submitting reports or some mechanism for financial accountability, often it is best if a liaison is assigned to the partnership who is at least of equal status. Then the reporting is from one person of status to another. However, some agencies do not exercise care in this area. They ask a male of high status to send expense and reimbursement reports to a mid-level person or female accountant in another culture. The indigenous partner feels demeaned and disrespected, so getting the person to complete the reports is like pulling teeth. The accountant feels disrespected as well. Why set up a system that is prone to difficulties in so many areas? Status is a key area that needs to be examined as accountability and reporting processes are developed in cross-cultural ministry partnerships. If reporting processes are designed well, it will often result in a higher level of fiscal integrity.

IMPLICATIONS FOR CROSS-CULTURAL PARTNERSHIPS

Loss of face if funds are not shared when needed. Over the years the most common reason I have seen partnerships disintegrate is because one partner, often in a collectivistic culture, chooses to use funding for purposes other than those designated by the donor. They often do this because of the incredible pressure they are incurring in their community. By virtue of their position, and because others in the community know that they have funds under their purview, pressure is exerted on them to take action in conjunction with their status to meet a pressing need. At times, if they do not meet the need, the loss of face will be so great it will put in jeopardy their ability to minister effectively in the community. Yet they know that their foreign partner will likely be upset as well. They have to balance which outcome is worse, a loss of face and standing in the community or the loss of future funds from a foreign donor. Often they fear the loss of face more.

This is not an unlikely or unpredictable scenario. It has happened many times in many different parts of the world. We need to recognize that partners in collectivistic cultures will indeed face this pressure at some time or other. Why not therefore take proactive steps at the outset of the partnership formation and think through the scenarios that might happen? From the beginning, pull together different types of partners so at least someone is able to meet these types of needs when they arise. Another option is to form some type of humanitarian fund with a donor designation that is broad enough to meet needs in the community without violating a ministry's tax-exempt purpose. Thought needs to be invested in this scenario *before* it happens. Face and status issues play a big role in many cultures. Everyone will benefit if there is a safe space to dialogue about it.

Creating effective feedback loops. Because of the role of power and face in cultures, it is very likely that you might receive a proverbial yes to all your ideas. Often simply coming as a foreigner with funding will cause others to view you as a person of high status. It would cause a substantial loss of face for a person of lower status to directly contradict a person of higher status and explain that his or her idea will not work. This innate "obliging style"[7] can create significant problems when it occurs, for key information is never brought to the forefront for consideration.

A way to acknowledge this reality and still be able to get the information you need is by creatively forming feedback loops that work in conjunction with the culture. For instance, create a way a lower-status person could pass on comments to someone else within the system or organization in a way that would not cause such a loss of face. This needs to be considered and developed differently in each context, for the nature of people and how and when they communicate displeasure or disapproval changes in each context and culture. But if time is taken to develop this, it will help to resolve the problem of the proverbial yes. Cross-cultural partners will then have the full scope of information they need to make effective decisions in a timely manner.

Adapting the style and function of meetings. Because of issues of status, it is necessary to exercise great care with regard to how or if you involve yourself in formal meetings. The context of Art's story was Asia. In that part of the region, votes are only taken in board meetings when true consensus has been reached through a series of earlier informal discussions and private gatherings. Only in that informal setting is it acceptable to raise questions, critiques and differing opinions. As those are heard and addressed, then a true consensus can be reached. Only when this processes is followed does a unanimous vote in a public meeting mean what it appears to mean. In other places people might feel uncomfortable disagreeing in public.[8] In other locations, the status issue might be such a significant barrier that it is better if a foreign partner is not even at the meeting.[9]

Acknowledging status in gift giving. Chapter two addressed how gifts in collective societies form a type of invisible bond of obligation between the giver and receiver. Accepting gifts can act as an informal type of contract whereby all those in that context feel the receiver is granting a promise to help with future needs. This is a distinct reality for many people working in other cultures. However, there is another component of gift giving that intersects with this issue. One student explains, "I constantly offered to do things for Boli Zhiang that he graciously refused. One time, I offered to get his computer fixed for free. He thanked me profusely yet had his computer fixed at a store. I was confused and troubled by this. Then his friend explained that to be in my debt, without any obvious means of returning the favor, would be, for him, a loss of face because he was ten years older than me. This meant that if I wanted to do something nice for him, I had to arrange for him to help me in some way."[10] Many going on short-term mission trips are most likely to misunderstand the impact of their generosity. It is noble to want to help others. However, how we go about doing it needs to be contextualized and exercised with great care. Otherwise the gift itself might embarrass and demean the person we want to help.

Looking past visits alone for the full story. In both Africa and Asia I have heard stories of Western missionaries or short-term mission teams arriving to help a church. As soon as people learn that the foreigners are coming, more people than ever attend the gathering. An Africa colleague said that he might skip church but if the missionary was in town, everyone went. In other congregations, on a typical Sunday there might be twenty or thirty people present. But when the overseas visitors come, hundreds attend. The foreign guest or short-term team might be led to believe that the church is growing and flourishing. However, people might be coming just so the pastor is not embarrassed. For if he looks good, more funds will come from abroad and the community as a whole will benefit. Or the large number of people attending can be in essence an attempt to show honor and hospitality to these foreign guests. They might do this out of the kindest of intentions because they feel it would be embarrassing for foreign guests to come from afar and only see twenty people in a church building.

Some partners base the success of their partnership ministry on the people they meet during these visits and the number of people attending church on those dates. They return home and explain how much the church is growing and how more funds need to be sent. However, they do not realize that the reason so many people attended was often the result of status issues, honor or saving face, and not because the church is truly growing and more people are coming to Christ. For this reason, it is important to have more than just personal visits as a way to gauge if or whether the partnership goals are being reached. Otherwise we can deceive ourselves that our partnership is fostering incredible church growth when no real growth has ever occurred.

Do people see you using funds carefully? Many Majority World partners are utterly amazed and confused that Western leaders will make a huge fuss over getting detailed accounting records for $5,000 sent abroad, all the while they seem to waste so much money in their own countries on things that do not seem wise or fruitful for the kingdom of God. Massive building programs frequently fall in this category. K. P. Yohannan writes, "A friend in Dallas recently pointed out a new church building costing $74 million. While this thought was still exploding in my mind, he pointed out another $7 million church building going up less than a minute away. These extravagant buildings are insanity from a Third World perspective. The $74 million spent on one new building here could build nearly fifteen thousand average-sized churches in India. The same $74 million would be enough to guarantee the evangelization of the whole state—or even some of the smaller countries in Asia."[11]

This comment puts into perspective what other non-Western partners are thinking as well. We want honesty, integrity and sacrifice on the part of our non-Western partners. We want them to be meticulously good stewards of the funds we give to them. However, are we applying that same standard of excellence, care and stewardship to the funds God is entrusting to us? Are we sending a message by how we live our lives that is congruent with what we are requiring of others?

Are all your processes sending the same message? A friend from Africa told me a story that highlights the importance of these issues. He and a team of local leaders were overseeing a community development project. Their council had been careful to budget the amount needed for the project. However, his country's currency fluctuated against the Euro, creating a sizable excess of funds. The project was completed as outlined, and it came in under budget. My friend approached the Western funding agency about the excess remaining but the person in their home office said, "Do not bother us about that. It will mess up our accounting if you send us back money. Use it for something else."

My friend said this sent all kinds of mixed messages about accountability, and it created great strife within the team of African leaders. Everyone on the council had serious personal and family needs, yet they were working together to better the community. Any of them could have used it for their own personal benefit. However, what was integrity in this situation? My friend said the council held on to the money for a while as they were fearful that someone else from the agency would ask for the money back, and they would later be blamed for spending it. After a significant lapse in time, the council voted on another community development project that had a similar outcome as the first, and they used the funds for this. My friend said from this point on, those African leaders laughed when this Western agency "talked" about accountability. The agency's processes spoke far more than the words used by a program manager or community development liaison.

Often there is a prejudice in the West that the non-Western world is corrupt and unfaithful with funds. Over the years I have found that to be an unfair and unjust analysis. I think it comes from our unwillingness to see the whole picture of what we are communicating abroad. Yes, there is room for non-Western leaders to grow in the area of financial accountability. However, there is also room for Western churches and mission agencies to improve as well. One way we can help foster this growth is to do a thorough analysis of all the church's or agency's processes to be sure they are communicating the same, consistent message. When our actions truly model our words, there will be far less misunderstanding and confusion in the area of financial accountability.

CONFUSING BEHAVIORS

If we want to work effectively across cultures, it is critical to understand how face, status and context affect communication. However, a few additional areas cause a great deal of confusion for partners as well. We will look at these in the next chapter.

Other Confusing Issues

There are other dimensions of culture that can confuse cross-cultural ministry partners. It is important to understand them so we do not inadvertently blame one another or dismiss actions as being inferior. Each has been shaped and formed in contexts where the practices make a great deal of sense. If we can grasp the reasons behind the actions, we will have the foundation of respect needed for dialogue. And it will only be in that place of respectful dialogue where we will begin to find the grace and creativity to meet the challenges we face.

How We View Rules

One of these core elements or dimensions of culture has to do with rules. If we are from a culture steeped in democratic values, we tend to be more absolute in our view of rules, and we feel all must carry them out fairly and consistently. However, much of the world does not function this way. They feel relational connections mean they are not bound by the same rules. Just as we saw in the last chapter that "rank has its privileges," so also do relational ties.

Defining terms. In social science literature, *universalism* and *particularism* are the terms that deal with this phenomenon. For many in ministry, these are new terms. Greg Storti, a cross-cultural trainer and consultant, explains that universalism represents an overall worldview where "there are certain absolutes that apply across the board, regardless of circumstances or the particular situation. What is right is always right. Whenever possible, you should try to apply the same rules to everyone in like situations. To be fair is to treat everyone alike and not make exceptions for family, friends, or members of your in-group. . . . While life isn't necessarily fair, you can make it more fair by treating everyone the same."[1] He explains that particularism is a worldview that believes "how you behave in a given situation depends on the circumstances. What is right in one situation may not be right in another. You treat family, friends, and your in-group members the best you can, and you let the rest of the world take care of itself. (Their in-groups will protect them.) . . . In any case, no one expects life to be fair. Personal feelings should not be laid aside but rather relied upon."[2]

Cultural roots. Both perspectives evolved through a context where, in that place and time, each unique way of viewing the world worked best. If there is a good infrastructure and lots of employment opportunities in a culture, it is logical that abilities more than relationships should determine if or whether a person gets hired. If the employment rate is only 50 percent and there is an overall sense of "limited good," it is logical that people will rely deeply on personal networks to get their needs met. And as one gives to another, it is natural to reciprocate.

Fons Trompenaars and Charles Hampden-Turner, international business consultants, write, "Business people from both societies will tend to think each other corrupt. A universalist will say of particularists, 'they cannot be trusted because they will always help their friends' and the particularist, conversely, will say of the universalists, 'you cannot trust them; they would not even help a friend.'"[3] So for the exact same reason we can end up distrusting one another.

DEALING WITH AMBIGUITY

Our ability to understand ambiguity is also critically important in cross-cultural partnerships. An Ethiopian stated, "Americans are very explicit; . . . they want a 'yes' or a 'no.' If someone tries to speak figuratively, Americans become confused."[4] Speaking on behalf of my own cultural heritage, I can tell you in all honesty that we truly do not mean to be so dense. I know the feeling of being in cross-cultural situations and sensing "in my gut" that something was just said or done that had profound significance. However, since I was not from that cultural heritage, I did not "get" it. I was never trained to have to "get" it. I never had to develop this skill. It does not come intuitively or naturally to me because my cultural heritage as a whole has a very low tolerance for ambiguity.

Understanding the concepts. Research done by the Hofstedes is helpful for cross-cultural partners to understand. They explain that in some cultures, "What is different is dangerous."[5] People "feel threatened by ambiguous or unknown situations. This feeling is, among other things, expressed through nervous stress and a need for predictability: a need for written and unwritten rules."[6] Research indicates that "some cultures are more anxious than oth-

For some the partnership agreement is the final word, and for others it is simply a general guide or starting place showing the most initial expectations for the relationship.

ers."[7] In other cultures, "uncertainty is a normal feature of life and each day is accepted as it comes."[8] Things do not need to be spelled out in detail in advance. People are comfortable with ambiguity and not knowing all the facts.

PARTNERSHIP AGREEMENTS AND REPORTING REQUIREMENTS

The very way some people seek to partner with individuals or organizations in other cultures is to design clear, concise and very detailed partnership agreements and mandatory reporting requirements. There is also a strong belief that unclear expectations only lead to problems. The governments to whom these leaders have to report are even less tolerant of ambiguity. The Hofstede research confirms that "from a cultural point of view, accounting systems in organizations are best understood as uncertainty-reducing rituals, fulfilling a cultural need for certainty, simplicity, and truth in a confusing world."[9]

If Gene comes from a culture that seeks to reduce or significantly lessen ambiguity and Jesse is quite comfortable and prefers to work differently, it can cause serious problems. Gene will expect to get information that he needs. If his queries are met with vague and ambiguous answers, his first instinct will be to begin distrusting Jesse. This will happen even if Jesse is wholly faithful and trustworthy. The reason this happens is that in many cultures the desire for full disclosure and full information is so innate in our being, in our culture and in our personal experiences, the only time people tend to be unwilling to disclose information is if they have something to hide or if they did something wrong.

However, for many cross-cultural partners like Jesse, they may be giving vague or ambiguous answers simply because that is the normal way they work and communicate. There might be no wrongdoing or impropriety. Yet if a Majority World partner like Jesse persists in giving vague answers, it will seriously hurt the partnership. The reason is that Gene and other partners coming from cultures that are not comfortable with ambiguity not only have to satisfy their own questions, they also have to account to governmental authorities who are even less tolerant of ambiguity.

To provide insufficient or inadequate information causes partners like Gene to be in a vulnerable position. They could be held criminally negligent and incur a prison term if there is too much ambiguity and accounting information is too vague. At the least, there is the serious possibility that Gene could lose his job and his credibility with donors, which he needs to be effective in ministry.

Why is it necessary to understand this dynamic? If we do not, we will continue to fight over which way of working is better. In reality, I think we see advantages and disadvantages to both ways of "being." We also see passages in Scripture that talk of care and planning (Proverbs 3:6; Luke 22:7-13; Acts 19:21) and those that mention taking no care for tomorrow (Matthew 6:25-34; Luke 10:38-42; James 4:13-16). The way we get through this is by understanding that neither partner is acting out of destructive or harmful motives. Instead, each of us has been deeply affected by our own cultural heritage, and we have to be able to function in a way that enables us to have the confidence of those who give us funding for ministry. Otherwise, resources will dry up and the work of the kingdom will be hindered.

PERSPECTIVES ABOUT TIME

How cross-cultural partners view time can also cause confusion. Edward Hall is often referred to as the father of inter-cultural studies. He has done extensive research over the years about how a culture's perception of time influences behavior. He explains that "time is so thoroughly woven into the fabric of existence that we are hardly aware of the degree to which it determines and coordinates everything we do. . . . By scheduling, we compartmentalize; this makes it possible to concentrate on one thing at a time, but it also reduces context. . . . The rules apply to everything except birth and death."[10] He explains that this worldview is called a monochronic orientation to time. For people coming from these types of cultures, time is "something fixed in nature, some ever-present part of the environment, just like the air we breathe. . . . That it might be experienced in any other ways seems unnatural and strange."[11] For people with a monochronic worldview, time is quite simply a commodity. It is an asset that should not be wasted or squandered. Craig Storti expounds on this perspective when he writes, "time is the given and people are the variable."[12] Schedules and deadlines are critical, and anything that gets in the way is a nuisance.

Another worldview is the polychronic orientation to time. Edward Hall explains that it "stresses involvement of people and completion of transactions rather than adherence to present schedules. Appointments are not taken as seriously, and as a consequence, are frequently broken. . . . Time is seldom experienced as "wasted," and is . . . often sacred."[13] He explains that "polychronic people are so deeply immersed in each other's business that they feel a compulsion to keep in touch. . . . Their involvement in people is the very core of their existence."[14] Storti explains that for polychronic people, "time is limitless and not quantifiable. There is always more time, and people are never too busy. Time is the servant and tool of people and is adjusted to suit the needs of people. Schedules and deadlines often get changed. . . . You always have to take circumstances into account and make adjustments. Strictly speaking, there's no such thing as an interruption."[15]

Advantages and disadvantages to both. A natural conclusion to a monochronic orientation is that it can enable people to accomplish a large number of tasks in an efficient way. It can create a sense of stewardship about how we spend our lives. If it influences people in this way, it can act as a catalyst so we are even more fruitful in ministry throughout our lives. It can lessen procrastination and cause things to happen more quickly. This orientation is not always helpful, though, because life does not run like a machine. It is not always predictable. It can cause us to compartmentalize in ways that cause us to make poor decisions. Hall explains that the "blindness of the monochronic organization is to the humanity of its members."[16]

Conversely, polychronism can create "a proliferation of small bureaucracies that really are not set up to handle the problems of outsiders. . . . One has to be an insider or have a 'friend' who can make things happen."[17] These are the shortcomings that many from monochronic worldviews observe in these cultures. However, there are extensive benefits to this way of seeing the world as well. Hall explains that "polychronic cultures are by their very nature oriented to people. Any human being who is naturally drawn to other human beings and who lives in a world dominated by human relations will be either pushed or pulled toward the polychronic end of the time spectrum. If you value people you must hear them out and cannot cut them off simply because of a schedule."[18]

Robert and Phillip were in a cross-cultural partnership that illustrates these conflicting worldviews. Robert came from a monochronic culture and Phillip was raised in a polychronic culture. When Robert arrived for a field visit, he had a set timeline in his mind. He wanted to get to several parts of the country to see the great work that Phillip's church-planting team was doing. Robert could only visit for one week because he had already used up most of his vacation time for the year. Since he was serving on the church mission committee, his involvement in the partnership was his volunteer service for the church. As the trip progressed, Robert grew frustrated and irritated with Phillip. Instead of getting to the different parts of the country, it seemed like Phillip was spending an inordinate amount of time talking with people and leaving intermittently to take long phone calls. Robert began questioning if Phillip was the best person to be leading the partnership initiative on the field. Phillip was getting frustrated too. He kept thinking, *Why is this American so impatient?*

APPLICATIONS FOR CROSS-CULTURAL PARTNERSHIPS

When it comes to these differing perspectives about time, there are many applications for those involved in cross-cultural partnerships. The most obvious application for those from monochronic orientations is a need to slow down! You do not have to work at warp speed. We are serving a God who has been at work among his people for thousands of years. If we enter cross-cultural partnerships with no margin of time, it will not go well. If we do not have much time for the visit, we either need to go a different time or we need to scale back our expectations. If we are not careful, our obsession about time will cause people to feel demeaned and used rather than appreciated and valued. Although some ministry outcomes will be met, other long-term damage will be done to the kingdom.

The second great need is to exercise mental discipline when certain things happen. When partnering with polychronic people, it is common that appointments and reporting deadlines will be missed, and distractions will occur when you meet in person. It is the nature of how they communicate and work with others. It is not a personal slight against you. It is also not a sign that they are ineffective in ministry. Quite the contrary! Some of these individuals have a track record of being exceedingly fruitful in ministry.

I would like to say that I am so spiritual that I always instantaneously believe the best about people. I would like to say that I am never thrown off when my expectations are not met. This is not true though. When financial reporting deadlines are missed, when partners constantly leave meetings to answer cell phones and when partners do not show up for important meetings, my gut reaction is negative. My initial instinct is to question their motives. Are they committed to this partnership? Do they even care about accountability? They seem to be spread so thin. Are they really doing a good job with this?

I realize after many years that because of my cultural heritage these will likely be the first thoughts that run through my head when I experience delays and broken deadlines. If I let my mind stay in that place, if I choose to dwell solely on those things, relationships will begin to deteriorate. Most of the time, thankfully, something else kicks in soon after these thoughts arise. I remember what I have learned about these different worldviews regarding time. I begin to step back and try to get a broader perspective. And I do not just stay in my own world. I start communicating to learn what is happening in my partner's world.

It is in this moment that I learn the true situation. I find out that distant relatives arrived from out of town unexpectedly and that has thrown off a leader's schedule. A spouse has been in the hospital for over a week with a bad case of malaria. Riots broke out and it has been too dangerous to get to the office. The twelfth typhoon of the season just blew through the area. It was a category four and has flooded the region. The road to the office is now four feet under water and the government has asked people to stay off the streets until the water level subsides. The excuses are not the old proverbial "the dog ate my homework" stories that children use when they decide to watch TV instead of doing their school assignments. On the contrary, these scenarios are often the daily realities faced by many Majority World partners in developing countries.

In much of the world, systems and infrastructures are vulnerable. Things do not proceed "like clockwork." People cannot plan and assume that what they set out to achieve will be accomplished in a timely manner. Often there are delays for extremely legitimate reasons. If cross-cultural partners jump to negative and careless conclusions, it will unnecessarily begin to destroy the partnership.

GROWING IN AWARENESS

Core cultural concepts that impact communication and behavior can be incredibly confusing if we do not take the time to understand them. However, other significant issues must be uprooted if we are going to partner well across cultures. We will look at these in the next section.

Part Two

UPROOTING
THE HARMFUL

THE PATH TO PREMATURE JUDGMENTS

When we feel disoriented, when things play out differently than we are expecting—on a conscious or unconscious level—we have to make sense of the experience. We begin asking all kinds of questions. Why did this happen? What does it mean? What was the person intending? The litany of questions continues until we arrive at a solution that seems to satisfy the internal questioning. Once a viable solution dawns in our minds, the uncomfortable feeling of disequilibrium leaves us, and we feel peaceful and able to move forward. The tricky thing about this process is it is often so innate and intuitive we frequently are wholly unaware it is even happening. Yet what evolves out of this "meaning making" process is so potent it has the capacity to spawn profound interpersonal growth or erode and deteriorate even the strongest of cross-cultural partnerships.

Meaning is determined by an inherent set of assumptions and beliefs formed throughout a person's life experience, so interpretations are unique and can vary greatly from person to person. It is the meaning assigned to experiences, not the experiences themselves, which determine if they will be transforming or deforming influences. A practical example of this can be seen as we watch two different women battling with breast cancer.

Sheila believes the reason she has breast cancer is because God does not love her and because life is unfair. She is filled with anger, rage and resentment. Over time she becomes more brittle and difficult to be with, and she hurts many of the people who love her most. Angie is stricken with the same disease. Angie also wrestles with how to make meaning of the experience. However, she chooses to believe God is allowing the trial to bring forth something of eternal good. She believes breast cancer is an "opportunity" God is giving her to share Christ with nurses and doctors and to minister to people she normally would never have had the opportunity to get to know. Over time, although she struggles with the discomfort of the disease and sorrow over having to say goodbye to loved ones, Angie is peaceful and cancer seems to transform her into an even better person.

Both are women with the same cancer. The meaning Sheila gives to the experience begins to deform her character and erode her personal relationships. The meaning Angie gives to it begins to bring life and transformation to her and others in her environment. Making meaning is a profoundly powerful thing!

How we "make meaning" has great implications for those involved in cross-cultural ministry partnerships. So often in cross-cultural work we assign meaning without thinking by making snap judgments about people and circumstances. These meanings are often subconscious, embedded in us because of our cultural heritage. If we never take time to objectively consider them, they will often carry us to unhealthy places and unhealthy outcomes. In essence, when habits of mind go unexamined, they "create limitations and form boxes of which we are unconscious and cannot, therefore, get beyond."[1]

Negative attribution happens when people do things that are not in line with what we expect. Although we have a choice to put their actions in one of three categories—right, wrong or different—we rarely put anything in that neutral ("different") category.[2] When we become confused by a partner's behavior, our initial human instinct is to attribute negative motives and intent as well. Once the unexpected behavior is deemed "bad" or "wrong," the tendency is to judge future behaviors in a negative light as well. This happens frequently in cross-cultural partnerships.

THREE EASY STEPS TO ERROR

Although there are many varieties and forms of attribution theory,[3] I think the form developed by Duane Elmer for cross-cultural workers is quite helpful. He outlines *negative attribution theory* in this way:

1. I am in a situation where my expectation is not met.

2. Instead of categorizing the behavior as neutral, I decide it is bad or wrong.

3. I then innately begin to infer negative intent and attributes to the person who did not act in accordance with my expectation.[4]

WHAT IS NEGATIVE ATTRIBUTION PHENOMENON?

Extensive research has been conducted in the area of attribution since the 1970s. Research in the area of cognition and attribution indicate that this phenomena is the "seeking or interpreting of evidence in ways that are partial to existing beliefs, expectations, or a hypothesis in hand."[5] It "connotes a less explicit, less conscious one-sided case building process. . . . The assumption that people can and do engage in case-building unwittingly, without intending to treat evidence in a biased way or even being aware of doing so, is fundamental to the concept."[6] It is as though when it occurs, people are only able to see what they are looking for "regardless of whether the patterns are really there."[7]

This phenomenon seems to be fueled by the reality that most people believe their own assessments are correct and unbiased. There does not seem to be awareness that attribution is based in beliefs and values that may or may not be applicable in different contexts. Research indicates that "the bias, by itself, might account for a significant fraction of the disputes, altercations, and misunderstandings that occur among individuals, groups and nations."[8]

HOW DOES NEGATIVE ATTRIBUTION WORK?

Researchers in the area of social psychology indicate that there are three stages to the process: "categorization (what is the actor doing?), characterization (what trait does the action imply?), and correction (what situational constraints may have caused the action?)."[9] There is a general misconception that one person's perception will be the same as another's because it operates "in about the same manner for everyone who shares their biology. People do not seem to believe (as most psychologists and philosophers do) that perceptions are achieved by higher order, cognitive processes and are thus influenced by one's idiosyncratic beliefs, attitudes and expectations."[10]

C. S. Lewis addresses the issue when he writes, "In our own case we accept excuses too easily; in other peoples' we do not accept them easily enough. As regards my own sins it is a safe bet (though not a certainty) that the excuses are not really so good as I think; as regards other men's sin against me it is a safe bet (though not a certainty) that the excuses are better than I think."[11] When it comes to money and missions, it is frequently as C. S. Lewis describes. Delays in financial reporting and not meeting some financial requirements might be attributable to truly noble reasons. However, often we simply "assume" the worst because we are confused and frustrated that our expectations are not met.

Why Do We Make Negative Attributions?

Researchers uncovered that "people make attributions because doing so enables them to achieve certain ends, for instance, to predict others and thereby control the extent to which others' behavior can affect them. . . . Finally, dispositional inferences afford the observer a culturally acceptable way of gaining a sense of control over her or his environment, and feelings of control, however illusory, may ultimately yield greater psychological benefits than would logically impeccable inferences."[12]

The research on attribution theory hits close to home for me. I would rather think the other person has the problem. This belief is far more pleasant than considering the uncomfortable truth that perhaps the attribution error is happening because I feel a need to control my environment. To be quite honest, I do not want to believe I am that immature as to feel the need to control things around me. Most people do not want to think of themselves as being controlling. However, we may feel internal disequilibrium when things turn out differently than we expected. As a result there is a strong psychological need to make sense of it, and to put a stop to that uncomfortable feeling as quickly as possible. Negative attribution gives us the ability to restore our equilibrium, and it helps us to feel less vulnerable in the world.

Under What Circumstances Is Negative Attribution Most Likely to Occur?

When we interact with a new culture. When we enter a new culture, we are extremely vulnerable to committing negative attribution. One study cites, "Spontaneous trait inference was particularly likely following practice with different behaviors and the same trait. These results show that practice with trait inferences contributes to the spontaneity of these inferences."[13] Because making meaning is intuitive, as we reach adulthood we do not realize the quantity of information we have learned about how to interpret human behavior. We see different behaviors following unique traits time and time again in our own culture, so we intuitively make similar assumptions when we view those same behaviors in a new context. However, the behavior in that new context might have a totally different meaning. This can get especially tricky when people are involved in cross-cultural partnerships in many contexts. Over time, leaders can gain a false confidence that they know how to work in the "global context." However, each place is unique, and how meaning is interpreted varies greatly from place to place.

When there are cohesive in-groups and out-groups. A recent analysis of the issue confirms that

> the relationship between the leader and the member is a critical moderator of the leader's attributions and subsequent behavior. The more a leader is empathetic with the member, sees the member as similar, respects and/or likes the member, the more likely the leader is to form "favorable" causal attributions for the member's performance (e.g., attributing success to internal causes and failure to external causes). The more removed the leader (e.g., the greater the power), the more likely the leader is to make "unfavorable" causal attributions about the member's performance.[14]

What this means is if there is a greater geographical distance between ministry partners and a significant cultural difference, there is a higher probability that behaviors will be misinterpreted. Any history of prejudice, paternalism or colonialism sets the stage as well, for often there can already be an innate "case building" taking place inside partners. When the out-group, whoever it might be, exhibits behaviors contradictory to the prejudice, it is often deemed to be an exceptional case or an anomaly instead of proof that the prejudice might be wholly unjustified.

In settings where projects and performance are being evaluated. Financial reporting is a mechanism by which partners measure the progress and effectiveness of programs. Recent research confirms that it is within this area of performance appraisals and evaluation where partners might especially benefit from the insights of attribution theory. Those evaluating others need to be especially aware and on guard.[15]

When there is no process for holding people accountable for their beliefs. This aspect of the research was also quite compelling. One study indicated that participants were far less likely to commit an attribution error if they knew they would be required to account for their opinions.[16] In other words, negative attribution can be greatly reduced if people are not permitted to speak prematurely or give a negative report about a partner unless they have adequate support and documentation for their opinion. By implementing such policy, the research indicates it will lessen the likelihood of negative attribution taking place.

When critical thinking is not required in the earliest stages. Most people tend to form a hypothesis or conclusion right away. Once they have formed this initial hypothesis, they do not consider other possibilities unless they are prompted or required to do so.[17] Research indicates that this flaw "can be reduced if people are asked to consider alternatives, but that they tend not to consider them spontaneously."[18]

When leaders and practitioners are busy and juggling many things. Attribution research also indicates that when people are busy and juggling many things, they are less able to access and utilize all the information they have stored in their minds. They might have the key pieces needed to make the best assessment. However, when the mind is busy and distracted with many things, there is limited capacity to utilize information well.[19]

In ministry there seems to often be what I would call a super-man complex. People always think they can do more and more and more. Most people in missions are wearing many hats and performing many different functions. This scenario makes us even more vulnerable to developing premature and inaccurate judgments and assessments.

FORMING CORRECT ASSESSMENTS

If we understand the mental process involved in making wrong assessments, we can better discern our own thought patterns. If we know how our thought process is working, it becomes easier to detect erroneous thinking before we damage relationships. In the next chapter we will examine how insights from this research can also help us as we seek to root out paternalistic attitudes in our ministries.

Paternalism Couched
as Accountability

Choose your metaphor carefully. The power of its dysfunction might be felt for generations!" This phrase haunts me. I do not know if I heard it before or if it was an original thought that came to me out of the utter frustration of this topic. I have not been able to locate the quote in my research. Either way, it seems to be an appropriate phrase to open our discussion on paternalism in missions.

The Bible uses numerous paternal metaphors. Believers are referred to as children of Abraham.[1] Paul speaks of Timothy as his son in the faith.[2] Paternal phrases can be comforting if used in the right context. In collective cultures familial titles are given to everyone. By knowing where we fit in a family, others are better able to determine our place in society.

The problem with the familial metaphors, however, arises when one person uses the term but the other person does not feel it is fitting. One person is referred to with a parental title and the other is their "child." The recipient of the lesser title experiences the term as a limitation in their life and ministry. A somewhat common scenario arises when a national partner is given a formal position of leadership but "unofficially" a foreign partner uses financial resources as a means to continue to control the ministry. Donor-designated funding is doled out only if the person conducts the ministry in exactly the same fashion as the "parent" deems to be appropriate.

HOW IS PATERNALISM DEFINED?

I attended an excellent conference in Canada where two men, one Native American and the other Caucasian, talked about the issue of paternalism in ministry. In their presentation they defined paternalism as "acting for the good of another person without the person's consent."[3] Another insight was that "paternalists advance peoples' interests (such as life, health or safety) at the expense of their liberty."[4] The *Merriam-Webster Dictionary* defines it as "a system under which an authority treats those under its control paternally (as by regulating their conduct and supplying their needs)."[5] I find these quotations fascinating because they paint the realities so often seen in the global mission movement.

In missions paternalism is often connected with colonialism, that period of time when foreign governments conquered and ruled over various parts of the world. The concept of colonialism can be found even in Christ's era as Caesar and Rome controlled that region of the Middle East (John 19:12-15). Under colonialism foreign powers determine how commerce and taxes are managed, how people are educated, and they usually invest funds for roads and other needed infrastructure. The problem that exists now is although foreign governments might not physically occupy an area, by their rules and power they are still controlling people from a far. Often their initiatives have the appearance of being altruistic, but they occur at the expense of peoples' liberties and freedom to make their own choices for their homeland. The common phrase used to describe this more recent phenomenon is neocolonialism.

In the book *Revolution in World Missions,* Yohannan describes what he has heard mission leaders say in the past. One distinctly commented, "'Our policy is to *use* the nationals to expand churches with our denominational distinctives.' The words 'use the nationals' rolled around in my mind. This is what colonialism was all about, and it is still what neocolonialism of most Western missions is all about. With their money and technology, many organizations are simply buying people to perpetuate their foreign denominations, ways and beliefs."[6] His statement struck a chord in me because often the result of paternalistic behavior is to cause another to wholly replicate our own behavior.

ROOTS OF SUPERIORITY

What often occurs in cross-cultural partnership is that the person coming from the more affluent or developed country assumes he or she knows what is best. For example, if Joshua graduates from an Ivy League undergraduate program and proceeds on to a renowned North American seminary, he is far less likely to genuinely listen to his indigenous partner. The education he has received has subtly and implicitly wired him to believe that he has the answers and he knows what is best for others. Another belief often follows that initial cognitive leap. Since Joshua knows what is best, and since he is a steward of church or mission funding, he will allocate money only to those "ideas" that are initially in sync with his own assumptions. He will frequently jump to and align himself only with those mission strategies and ministries that look like his own. Joshua does not mean to act out of neocolonialism. In fact, that is opposite of the values he espouses. Yet because of his culture, he will often behave this way without ever realizing it.

Nancy Adler gets at this tendency in her book *International Dimensions of Organizational Behavior.* Using slightly different termi-

nology, she writes, "Parochialism means viewing the world solely
through one's own eyes and perspective. . . . Americans speak
fewer foreign languages, demonstrate less interest in other cultures, and are more naïve in global business situations than the
majority of their trading partners."[7]

Duane Elmer writes, "Superiority cloaked in a desire to serve is
still superiority. It's not our words that count but the perception of
the local people who watch our lives and sense our attitudes."[8] He
later writes, "If you try to serve people without understanding them,
you are more likely to be perceived as a benevolent oppressor."[9]

Often as we work in cross-cultural ministry partnerships, as
the wealthy partners we assume that processes and procedures
will be followed according to "our way." There can be an inherent
sense of superiority that infects the tones and overtures of how we
work and how we make decisions. Only if this false sense of superiority is brought to the forefront can it be critically examined.
Otherwise, it will continue to disguise itself as some type of virtue
or be rationalized away by those who most need to change.

NO MARGIN FOR OTHERS TO MAKE MISTAKES AND GROW

Paternalistic thinking causes people to not let go of control, for
they feel others will not do as good a job as they would. When it
comes to money, it is the belief that only "we" will do it "right."
There is no margin for people to develop, make mistakes and
learn. Yohannan writes, "Part of the sin of pride is a subtle but
deep racism. As I travel, I often hear innocent-sounding questions
such as, 'How do we know that the native church is ready to handle the funds?' or 'What kind of training have the native missionaries had?' So long as such questions are based on a sincere desire
for good stewardship, they are commendable, but in many cases I
have found the intent of the questions are much less honorable.

Westerners refuse to trust Asians the way they trust their own people."[10] I feel this quotation squarely addresses how we can tell if accountability is morphing into paternalism. It is the heart of the person, not the act of seeking accountability itself, that determines if it is one or the other.

People often forget how much of a learning curve they have experienced. When it comes to fiscal management, it takes a long time to grow and know how to handle things well. Everyone who is a trained accountant spent time learning the profession, and part of that learning came from making mistakes. If we are only willing to hand something over to someone when they are "perfect," the transfer will never take place. For if we are truly honest with ourselves as we look in the mirror, we are not perfect either. The accounting profession is built on knowing that people will make mistakes because they are human. For that reason, good accounting processes always involve others checking our work and having controls so there are multiple people viewing everything. No partner is flawless. We all make mistakes. But those mistakes should be coaching points leading to growth and maturity.

When Belief Turns to Self-Fulfilling Prophecies

Many years ago an educational study was conducted called "Pygmalion."[11] In this study one group of teachers was told that their students were exceptionally bright. Their IQ scores were far superior to that of normal students. They might act lazy at times and they might act like they cannot understand or master some material, but this was not true. They had a profound capacity for learning and success. A different group of teachers was given a very different perspective on the students they would be teaching. They were told that their students were not so bright. Their IQ scores were not that high. Although some might show promise, in reality they would not have much capacity to learn or excel. What the two different groups of teachers did not know, however, was that the IQ scores and ability of their relative sets of students were the same. One group of students was not brighter or more gifted than the other. They were, for all practical measures, statistically equal.

Time went on and the results were stunning. The students working with teachers who believed in their abilities and capacities saw tremendous growth and success. The other students, well, not so much. After all, what did anyone expect? The study was stopped prematurely because the researchers felt it was too harmful for the children to continue. The first group continued to make incredible leaps in progress and growth. The second group was struggling even at its best moments. What was the difference? The students were the same. The difference arose squarely from what others thought or believed they could do. Low expectations on the part of those who were meant to be encouragers and trainers became self-fulfilling prophecies.

A meaningful corollary is present in missions when it comes to paternalism. National and Majority World missionaries are capable of extraordinary things. They can and are changing the world through the vitality of their faith and their extensive giftedness. The current trend is that the Majority World church is sending the greatest percentage of missionaries into the harvest field. This is good for world evangelism and global missions. However, if we do not shed false attitudes of superiority and false belief systems, we will be a hindrance in cross-cultural partnerships and we will be a hindrance to God's work in the world.

IS THERE A BETTER METAPHOR FOR MISSIONS?

John Rowell offers a healthier metaphor relating to money and missions.[12] He says the only healthy metaphor is one where we are all recognized as God's children, sitting at the same banquet table in Heaven. God, our heavenly Father, is over all of us. And, if the children from wealthier countries are sitting on one end of the table with all kinds of food and delicacies, and siblings on the other end of the table have no bread left on their side, it is wholly acceptable and right for them to ask us to pass a basket of bread to them![13] Perhaps in your part of the world the more appropriate analogy would be to pass the chicken, beans or rice. Whatever the food of choice, the image is quite clear. If we are all God's children eating from the same table, it is only normal for family members to share with one another because they love each other.

When Dogma Holds Us Back

The flip side of this coin is how indigenous partners choose to make meaning of the behavior of wealthy partners. Organizational theorist Peter Senge writes, "Our personal meaning starts to become incoherent when it becomes fixed. The incoherence increases when past meaning is imposed on present situations. As this continues, yesterday's meaning becomes today's dogma, often losing much of its original meaningfulness in the process."[14]

At times the knee-jerk reaction when financial accountability is involved is that it is "just another example of paternalism and neocolonialism." The meaning that might have been true in the past becomes the automatic meaning for the present, irrespective of whether or not such a judgment is true. In this current era, frequently it is not a true or accurate meaning. Let me explain.

I can attest to a reality that I have seen time and again over the last decade when I have been engaged in financial matters in the mission field. Most of my colleagues dislike having to spend time dealing with receipts and financial documentation. Most are busy.

They feel it is a nuisance. They think it is a disruption to their work, and in their hearts they do not want to do it. The only thing they dislike more is asking or requiring others to do it. However, they know that laws in the United States are extremely tight and grants coming from aid agencies such as CIDA and other organizations often require a lot of documentation to ensure that funding will continue. So for that reason alone, they comply and ask others to comply as well. That has been the reality of my experience, both within the Wycliffe family of organizations and as I work with countless people from other ministries and agencies as well. Maybe two to three percent of the people I know in ministry get some form of gratification out of complying with all these regulations and requiring others to comply. However, the vast majority of ministry leaders, missionaries, practitioners and pastors do not.

From what I have experienced, the majority of partners seeking this information do not want to be demeaning or controlling. They are doing it because they are required by law to do it. And if they do not, many donors and foundations will not give money to help with ministry efforts in the future. Because they want to see lives changed, they jump through the required legal hoops, as annoying and bothersome as they are at times.

The reality faced by many engaged in nonprofit agencies around the world is that even non-Western governments are becoming more concerned with fiscal integrity and accountability. After the fall of communism in Eastern Europe, there was much fraud when many nonprofit foundations were established. Consequently, many of these governments are now strict with any funding running through these types of agencies. Clearly, not all requests for financial documentation are based on paternalistic, neocolonialistic attitudes. If we choose to always assume that is the meaning for such actions, we will be treating others unfairly, and we will cause our cross-cultural ministry partnerships to deteriorate for no reason. It is more important to know the motivation and attitude behind the request, not the actual request itself.

THE COMPLEXITIES OF LIFE

Human beings and the world we inhabit are incredibly complex. Rooting out erroneous assumptions and beliefs can be hard work but it is well worth the effort. If we do not take time to address these, it is likely that partners from different cultures will wrongly judge one another. When this happens, damage is done to the kingdom of God and to the very people we seek to help. In the next chapter we will look at other common unintended consequences that can happen despite our good intentions.

6

Common Unintended Consequences

There is a phenomenon in life commonly referred to as the *law of unintended consequences.* The general gist is that, as we set out and try to actively resolve one problem, our solution unknowingly creates future problems. If you have ever done home remodeling, you might have seen this process at work and can appreciate how maddening it can be. My husband and I bought a "fixer-upper" that was marketed as a "handy-man's special." Those phrases mean we got a good price on the home, but it needed a great deal of work. Invariably whenever we try to remodel or improve any part of the house, there will always be at least one "unforeseen" problem that will arise because of the action we decided to take to "improve" our situation.

For example, we thought it would be good to have our bedroom floor refinished. The contractor we hired did a great job and at a very reasonable price. However, one of the selling features of the home was that it came with an excellent security system. A few days after this remodeling project was completed, we realized one of the workmen sanded through an electrical line, thus disabling the security system. We then had to get the security system fixed, and that repair was quite expensive.

We see the law of unintended consequences on a global scale all the time in foreign policy decisions. One vivid example is with Osama bin Laden. The U.S. military trained bin Laden and his men with state-of-the-art weaponry so they could hold back Russian forces invading Afghanistan during the Cold War. Although this "fix" sought to resolve one issue, on September 11, 2001, the law of unintended consequences became evident. Years later highly trained men under Osama bin Laden's leadership used their skills to attack Americans and obliterate the World Trade Center. Thousands of innocent lives were lost or forever changed.

The law of unintended consequences in missions raises an important question. Can we, in the midst of trying so hard to "do good," actually make a situation worse? Sadly, when it comes to global missions, some unintended consequences have become virtually predictable. With many churches and new organizations entering into cross-cultural ministry partnerships, it is important to examine common missteps. Such examination can shorten our learning curve. If we are going to be making mistakes in missions, we should at least be making new ones.

THE DEPENDENCY DEBATE

There is quite a debate in missiological circles about the issue of dependency and whether or not foreign leaders should partner with indigenous leaders and organizations at all. The fear is that it will create unhealthy dependency that will only cause people to be worse off in the long run. John Rowell[1] and Glenn Schwartz[2] each wrote a book taking different sides on the issue.

Rowell has been involved in fruitful cross-cultural partnerships in Bosnia for many years. He argues that believers should generously share financial resources with partners in other countries so greater outcomes can be realized in global missions. Schwartz has spent much of his ministry life in Africa, and some time in Latin America as well. He has seen financial giving work against the development and empowerment of a strong indigenous church and mission movement whereas Rowell has seen outside funding strengthen indigenous ministries. I will not be taking sides because I believe God's answers often lie somewhere in between the two polarizing views.

As I read these authors in-depth I kept sensing that often the answer is yes to both perspectives. Some might wonder, how can both be right? One supports partnering to help congregations build churches. The other argues that funding should never be given to help a congregation build a church. How then can you say you agree with both perspectives? I think the answer to these questions lies in understanding the context from which both authors are working. John Rowell's context is Eastern Europe, specifically Bosnia and the surrounding areas. In this part of the world, communism reigned for a long time. After the fall of communism, a gruesome civil and ethnic cleansing pervaded the region. After peace was restored and maintained, discussions about entering the European Union ensued. All of these circumstances, and the scarcity or plentiful nature of land, buildings, and supplies, greatly affect how difficult and expensive it is to build a church. In many parts of Africa where the weather is milder, land is more plentiful, and where churches can be constructed with supplies that are more readily attainable, it is often easier to fund building projects locally.

The heart of Schwartz's argument is that the "dependency syndrome has little to do with wealth or poverty. It has to do with the mentality on the part of both local people and the outsiders who try to help."[3] He feels we need to be careful not to see people as helpless or unable to develop on their own. He believes if we treat people this way, and assume they cannot do things, they will also start to believe they are powerless to address and overcome their own problems. And if the people themselves begin believing this lie, it will be the greatest disability of all.

External funding may weaken local incentives to give. I say external funding *may* weaken local incentives because external funding does not always weaken local incentives to give. Schwartz writes, "Part of the dependency syndrome has to do with the way we westerners solve problems. We solve problems with money. . . . The problem is that we westerners are often unable to separate the joy we get from giving from the unhealthy dependency that can result on the receiving end."[4] A problem arises out of this generosity. Schwartz writes, 'If money is that easy to get overseas, why do we work so hard to get it locally?' When local people come to that conclusion, they are choosing a short-term solution with long-term consequences."[5]

To these comments I say yes and amen. In the United States, for example, we are notorious for thinking if we just throw money at something, everything will be better. We often do this instinctively because internally we feel such great disequilibrium and heartache at the disparity of resources. We give quickly, almost out of instinct, because we want that uncomfortable and unpleasant feeling to go away. Instead of living with that tension and allowing it to be an irritation in our soul that over time can grow into a pearl of great wisdom, we short-circuit God's process for lasting transformation by giving money quickly and moving on.

Along this line Schwartz tells a story about a short-term mission trip participant. She came to work alongside a career missionary who was doing medical work and church planting. The career missionary was helping African believers to understand the difference their contribution could make in global missions. The African church took up a missionary offering and raised $61. This was a great increase from the $45 raised the year before. Everyone was deeply encouraged! The African believers planted a new church with the funds several kilometers away.

A problem arose, however, because of the well-intentioned short-term missionary. She had so much pity for the "poor Africans" that she depleted her entire savings account and gave them a donation of $6,800. From that point on, this African congregation quit giving local funds for mission. They put all their energy into finding out how they could get "more of that kind of money."[6]

Does external funding always serve as a de-motivator? I think it does not have to be. In some situations, I have seen foreign funding inspire the poor to give. In an experiment I was coordinating for Wycliffe International, I talked to Filipino colleagues who shared that a matching funds program inspired truly poor people in their context to give, as then even their small portions would automatically grow to be an even greater and more valuable contribution.[7] Many in NGOs and development organizations who I have talked to over the years have said if funding is combined with local giving, the results can be extraordinary. It goes back to what we choose to value. If money is the only contribution that is measured or seen, the picture can become quite distorted.

Foreign funding may weaken local incentive to act. Again, I believe the word *may* is the operative word in this statement. Schwartz writes that many local evangelists in Africa do not go into missionary work because they don't have a foreign sponsor. He explains that many people say evangelistic work is for the people who get "paid from overseas."[8] In some contexts he has witnessed that outside funding causes others to think they cannot take action on their own initiative or with their own resources.

Rowell's counterargument will be explored in greater depth as we consider issues of mutuality and sustainability in the next chapters. Suffice to say, this is an important issue to consider. However, I think more than just "foreign funding" is at play in determining whether there will be a disincentive to act and own ministry. It is often not the money, but how the money factors into who leads, who makes the decisions and who sets priorities for ministry. If these other factors are set up well, foreign funding is able to be a true blessing and not a disincentive for action.

Foreign funding may weaken local accountability structures. Schwartz has seen people frequently send foreign funding to a specific person. That leader or person rarely tells the church the scope of the gift given or provides a transparent accounting of how it is spent. When funding is given this way to a person, and there is no local accountability regarding how it is managed and utilized, I do believe foreign funding has the capacity to weaken local accountability structures.

I have heard several people comment on a similar phenomenon in various parts of the world. If a prominent pastor is committing adultery or involved in a serious sin, people remain silent. They fear the foreign partner who has a relationship primarily with that one specific leader will stop sending funding, and that could negatively affect many lives. For this reason, if we want foreign funding to be a blessing, we need to be sure we are not accidentally creating scenarios where local leaders no longer hold one another accountable. Organizations and churches can often avoid this unintended consequence if they choose to partner with an indigenous mission or elder board.

Behind the Buzzword *Dependency*

John Rowell argues that many people hide behind the "fear of creating dependency" as an excuse to not give sacrificially and generously.[9] This can be the case in various situations. However, I have seen it used in a different way. When I hear "fear of dependency" discussed in my own culture, I see something else. At times I feel it is used as a smoke screen for people being unwilling to make a long-term strategic commitment to a specific area of the world. In our individualistic culture there is a tendency for us to keep things from "sticking to us." We want to be "free." We want to respond when we want to respond. We want to give to whatever issue or cause makes us feel good at any given time. We do not want to feel trapped and tied to an issue that is no longer in the headlines. We want to go to those places and causes that are "high profile" at any given time. My concern when I hear of churches being afraid of creating dependency is that some times pastors and church leaders are not being honest about what is truly in their hearts. Before we can adequately address the issue of dependency, we also need to do some serious soul searching and address the role our own self-centeredness might be playing in the debate.

WHO DECIDES ABOUT DEPENDENCY?

When it comes to the issue of dependency, often Majority World leaders are not included in the discussion. Rowell alludes to this dynamic in his experiences. In countries like the United States people often just decide not to give for fear of creating unhealthy dependency. It appears to me as though there can be a polarizing mentality, as though there are only two extremes in the equation. You can either choose not to give at all or you can give and risk really messing up peoples' lives for generations to come. Is there no middle ground? Are there no other solutions than this? When I talk to cross-cultural friends and partners, they feel such a simplistic approach to a complex issue is unwise. They feel there are many ways to still partner and give financially while lessening or wholly eliminating the issue of unhealthy dependency. When people in affluent countries decide not to give, indigenous partners feel they are being treated as children, excluded from the dialogue and disrespected as colleagues. Their insights are needed in each context and in each endeavor to determine the best way to proceed.

OTHER UNINTENDED CONSEQUENCES

Although unhealthy dependency is a serious unintended consequence that we need to carefully consider, it is not the only one. I believe two other issues need to be carefully considered as well. If not, it will be to the detriment of our ministry partners.

Foreign funding may divide the church. During World War II, Shantung Compound was a detention center in China.[10] The situation in this compound was different from many others during the war. As a whole the detainees were treated fairly and were instructed to create their own society, so to speak. They dealt with their own issues regarding space, housing, education, medical care and distribution of resources. The Japanese authorities only stepped in when necessary. Since the detainees were so diverse and highly educated, the camp became a microcosm in the study of sociology and cultural anthropology.

One prisoner, Langdon Gilkey, later wrote of his experiences and described the camp. He said, "Next to space, food was the necessity in very short supply. We never reached the point of starvation, but supplies were meager at best and hunger was always with us."[11] The author then explained that an amazing thing happened. A small supply of care packages was sent to the camp from the U.S. Red Cross for American citizens. Although Americans comprised only a small portion of all the detainees, the packages made them incredibly rich in comparison. The packages meant that the Americans would not be hungry for weeks, while inmates of other nationalities would surely suffer.[12]

Later an enormous shipment of Red Cross care packages arrived from the United States and all the detainees wondered what would happen, as for the first time it was now possible for every detainee to receive a container of goods. Gilkey wrote,

> Two days later the Japanese authorities posted a notice which seemed to settle the issue to everyone's apparent satisfaction. The commandant . . . proclaimed that the parcels were to be distributed to the entire camp the next day at 10 A.M. Every American was to receive one and one-half parcels; every other internee, one parcel. This ingenious distribution was possible because there were 1,550 parcels for a camp of 1,450 persons, 200 of whom were Americans. . . . Universal good will flooded the camp; enthusiasm for American generosity was expressed on every hand. Our morale and our sense of community had climbed swiftly from an all-time low to an all-time high.[13]

However, seven Americans protested. They demanded to see authorization from a Japanese or American official saying it was permissible to give U.S. Red Cross parcels to non-Americans. These protestors wanted to split all parcels just among the 200 Americans. The Japanese guard running the internment camp lost face, and he stopped any distribution until a higher authority was consulted. In the end the final decision was that each person, no matter what his or her nationality, would receive only one parcel. Any remaining parcels would be sent to another internment camp.

As Gilkey reflected on the experience he wrote,

> Wealth is a dynamic force that can too easily become demonic—for if it does not do great good, it can do great harm. . . . Had this food simply been used for the good of the whole community, it would have been an unmitigated blessing in the life of every one of us. But the moment it

threatened to become the hoarded property of a select few, it became at once destructive rather than creative, dividing us from one another and destroying every vestige of communal unity and morale.[14]

I include this story and the author's analysis of the situation not to promote a communist or socialistic agenda, for we see in Scripture that God gives people the right to make their own choices about how to share or utilize personal resources (Acts 5:3-4; 2 Corinthians 9:6-8). However, this transition from "need to greed" is so common throughout the world, the divisive nature of "giving" has to be addressed. At a conference Sherwood Lingenfelter addressed this somewhat predictable outcome. He felt cross-cultural ministry partners need to prepare each other for this inevitable reality. He recommended that partners do some brainstorming of what types of sinful behaviors might happen if additional funding is received, and then role play various scenarios so people are not caught off guard when it occurs. He talked about the need to help people get in touch with their "default culture" and think through how they might respond differently.[15]

Daniel Goleman has done extensive research in the area of emotional intelligence training.[16] Emotional intelligence research provides a natural parallel to the development of cultural intelligence. Both forms of intelligence require learning how to function in new and different ways that are more appropriate and helpful in a given setting. What Sherwood Lingenfelter proposes seems to coincide well with these research findings. Role playing gives people a safe environment to try out new behaviors and responses. As these are acted out, they would create new pathways in the brain circuitry. We have to be willing to address the fallen nature of humankind and not enter cross-cultural ministry partnerships with naiveté. Giving can foster true blessing or profound dysfunction and strife.

Foreign funding may place your indigenous partner at great risk. Last, I want to look at the issue of risk that indigenous partners often face by working with Western partners or wealthy partners from non-Western countries. I have known of people being kidnapped and held for ransom because others in that context realized they were associated with a foreign mission or with wealthy donors abroad. Other times I have heard of churches and agencies not adhering to the intense pleas of Majority World partners to protect their identities. When this is mishandled, these incredibly gifted and fruitful indigenous partners can be singled out by oppressive government leaders for detainment or torture.

Cross-cultural ministry partnership is not a game. We cannot approach things willy-nilly in sloppy and careless ways. We need to be astute, and we need to adhere to the cautions and requests of those working in other contexts. We need to protect them as best we can so their association with us does not harm them, their ministries or their families. We might not always be able to keep this unintended consequence from occurring, and at times something as extreme as martyrdom might strengthen the global church and the mission movement abroad. However, woe to us if we are the stumbling block when it was never God's intent! We will be held accountable for our promotional pieces, web communications and speaking engagements that highlight the work of our partners and the ministry we have together.

SO WHAT DO WE DO?

It can be quite daunting to know what to do in such a complex world. Perhaps we should just hide our wealth under a rock? There it will not do any harm—right? But we see in the parable of the talents that is not likely to be a good option either (Matthew 25:14-30). We live in a world where there is potential for giving to cause profound dysfunction, strife and disabling dependency. Yet we also see passages like the one about Lazarus in Luke 16:19-31. Lazarus used to sit at the gate of the rich man and, as the story progresses, both men die. The angels carry Lazarus to Abraham's bosom. The rich man died and awoke in hell. The rich man faced this sentence not because he was ever overtly mean to Lazarus, but simply because he never cared about his desperate situation. For this reason, choosing to do nothing about those in need around the world does not seem to be an option for those who say they love God and are followers of Christ.[17]

Partnering well will not come naturally for many of us. Yet it is possible. We can learn, we can grow, and we can develop in ways that are a blessing to the global church. We cannot weather these issues in our own strength and wisdom. But we can learn about dependency. It does not have to become dogma or jargon that shuts down creativity and thought. Instead, the issue of dependency and the law of unintended consequences can serve as tutors, keeping us humble. The complexities can lead us to even deeper dependence and reliance on God and on one another so that we discover better ways of working.

Looking Ahead

Until now we have taken time to examine common reasons why people do not partner well across cultures. Without this foundation we will fall into the same traps and make the same mistakes as others who have gone before us. We will now build upon this foundation and examine how we can partner in better ways.

Part Three

PARTNERING IN
BETTER WAYS

Biblical Foundations
for Accountability

Thy word is a lamp unto my feet, and a light unto my path.

—Psalm 119:105 kjv

Throughout the world there are many different beliefs about how money and resources should be utilized and accounted for. We have spent time looking at the different dimensions of culture and the worldviews they foster regarding money. I think it is also helpful to look into Scripture and examine an important question. Does God really care that much about financial accountability? Although we cannot to delve into an analysis of the 2,350 verses of Scripture that address money and resources,[1] let's reflect on a few compelling passages.

The First Donor-Designated Asset

The Genesis account of creation is provocative.[2] As God fashioned humanity, he gave Adam and Eve scores of spectacular things to enjoy. The Garden of Eden by all accounts appears in Scripture to be a virtual paradise. Adam and Eve oversaw God's creation, named the animals, and were well equipped to enjoy a happy and fulfilling life forevermore. There was one catch though. Genesis 2:16-17 says, "The LORD God commanded the man, saying, 'From any tree of the garden you may eat freely; but from the tree of the knowledge of good and evil you shall not eat, for in the day that you eat from it you will surely die.'" God gave them everything to enjoy with one exception; he had a different intention for one of his resources. The tree of the knowledge of good and evil was set aside for a different purpose. For that reason, they were not to eat from it or use it for their personal benefit.

Sadly, the next chapter in the book of Genesis provides a glimpse of what occurred when Adam and Eve chose to dishonor that first "donor designation" and use the resource for their own purposes. Although their relationship with God was not wholly severed, it was deeply damaged. It would take thousands of years before Christ's redemptive purposes would be achieved, and even then life would not be as good on earth as it had been prior to this act of rebellion. From the day they ate the fruit, Adam and Eve set into motion a decaying process in their bodies. They would no longer live eternally on earth, nor would they experience unhindered communion with the One who made them. Instead, a diametrically different course was forged, and it would be riddled with murder, heartache and suffering.

God seemed to take this act quite seriously. He was very clear from the outset that this resource was set aside for a different purpose. He was not vague about it. When God's donor designated purpose was dishonored, he did not merely turn his head and "pretend" it did not happen. Things changed as a result of the act, and it has had long-term implications for all of us, even to this very day.

TAKING FROM THE TREASURY

The sad story of Achan also sheds light on the issue of accountability with regards to designated assets. Joshua and the children of Israel had consecrated themselves and were on the cusp of finally entering the Promised Land. Standing before them was the city of Jericho. God promised to work on their behalf to give them the city. But he had an important provision. Joshua states it clearly prior to the attack by saying in Joshua 6:18-19, "But as for you, only keep yourselves from the things under the ban, so that you do not covet them and take some of the things under the ban, and make the camp of Israel accursed and bring trouble on it. But all the silver and gold and articles of bronze and iron are holy to the LORD; they shall go into the treasury of the LORD." The trumpets were sounded, the shout went out, and the walls collapsed before them. They seemed careful to obey God's commands, all except one of them.

Scripture indicates that the Lord was with Joshua and his fame spread throughout the land. When it was time for the next military advance, Joshua and his leaders felt it was not necessary to send a large group of soldiers. Instead, approximately three thousand were sent. However, all were forced to flee before their enemies, and thirty-six of their own men were slaughtered (Joshua 7:3-5). After this defeat, Joshua offered this lament:

> Alas, O LORD God, why did You ever bring this people over the Jordan, only to deliver us into the hand of the Amorites, to destroy us? If only we had been willing to dwell beyond the Jordan! (Joshua 7:6-7)

Joshua continues the lament until God responds:

> Rise up! Why is it that you have fallen on your face? Israel has sinned, and they have also transgressed My covenant which I commanded them. And they have even taken some

of the things under the ban and have both stolen and deceived. Moreover, they have also put them among their own
things. Therefore the sons of Israel cannot stand before their
enemies; they turn their backs before their enemies, for they
have become accursed. I will not be with you anymore unless you destroy the things under the ban from your midst.
. . . In the morning then you shall come near by your tribes.
And it shall be that the tribe which the LORD takes by lot
shall come near by families, and the family which the LORD
takes shall come near by households, and the household
which the LORD takes shall come near man by man. It shall
be that the one who is taken with the things under the ban
shall be burned with fire, he and all that belongs to him,
because he has transgressed the covenant of the LORD, and
because he has committed a disgraceful thing in Israel.
(Joshua 7:10-12, 14-15)

We see that the next morning things transpired just as God
predicted. Lots were cast, sifting from the great numbers of people down to the exact man who had transgressed the ban. Joshua
inquired of Achan, "My son . . . tell me now what you have done.
Do not hide it from me." So Achan answered Joshua and said,
"Truly, I have sinned against the LORD, the God of Israel, and this
is what I did: when I saw among the spoil a beautiful mantle
from Shinar and two hundred shekels of silver and a bar of gold
fifty sheckels in weight, then I coveted them and took them; and
behold, they are concealed in the earth inside my tent with the
silver underneath it" (Joshua 7:19-21). They searched his tent
and it was as he had stated. All that was with Achan, his oxen
and sheep and donkeys along with his sons and daughters, were
destroyed that day.

It is a profoundly sad and moving story, but one from which

we can gain important insights. First, we see that God took this very seriously. Amidst the victory and all the actions of thousands upon thousands of people, he noticed one act, one transgression. The funds were supposed to go into the treasury, which would benefit the whole community and would be managed by those leading the children of Israel. This person sought in essence a micro-advantage for himself and for his family. Not only did his immediate family suffer for it, his animals were killed as well as thirty-six innocent soldiers. When we take what is supposed to be kept in God's storehouse or treasury, when we covet and take what God never said was rightfully ours, it harms the whole community. The end result is not good, and God indeed sees.

GOD'S FEELING ABOUT TWO DISHONEST DONORS

Another sobering lesson about how God views fiscal integrity and accountability is in the New Testament account of Ananias and Sapphira. After Christ's resurrection, the church was growing exponentially. Spectacular conversions were taking place. Scripture indicates that God was doing amazing miracles in their midst, and a tremendous love was prevailing within this new Christian community. People even ceased acting like their belongings were their own. Instead, owners of houses and lands would sell them and bring the proceeds of the sales and lay them at the apostles' feet so there were resources to meet the many needs.

We do not know the full scope of what possessed Ananias and Sapphira to devise such a plan amidst such a revival. They seemed to want the praise and glory attributed to those who were giving so sacrificially. They sold a piece of property, held some of the proceeds back for themselves, and laid the rest at Peter's feet. First Ananias came by himself before the apostle. Peter sensed he was lying and said in Acts 5:3-4, "Ananias, why has Satan filled your heart to lie to the Holy Spirit and to keep back some of the price of the land? While it remained unsold, did it not remain your own? And after it was sold, was it not under your control? Why is it that you have conceived this deed in your heart? You have not lied to men but to God." Scripture says that as Ananias heard these words, he fell over dead. They carried his body away. Later his wife arrived. Peter asked her if they had shared the full proceeds of the sale of the land with the church. She lied as well. He verbally confronted her sin and she also fell over dead.

What is going on here? There was no church-sanctioned communal living requirement. Peter made it clear as he spoke to Ananias that he was not obligated to sell any land for the church. Nor was he obligated to share the full price of any recently sold lands with the church. It was wholly his right to hold back part of the sum and make a partial contribution. But what did Ananias and Sapphira do? They were wealthy donors, and they pretended that they were "giving it all" for the kingdom. They gave the appearance of making great sacrifices when they were not making a great sacrifice. Instead of being authentic, genuine and transparent, they put forward an image that simply was not true.

The remarkable thing to me about this passage is that God cared so much! It is the only place in the New Testament where we see God smiting and killing people on the spot. From all accounts, it is pretty apparent that he abhorred this sin. He felt it would harm the community. Amidst the birth of the Christian church, miracles, signs, extensive numbers of new converts, God turned aside from all the successes and honed in on this one financial sin. He was not too busy or consumed with ministry to deal with it. Instead, from all practical accounts, it became his top priority. He did not seem to think "transparency" was an issue solely for the recipient of financial gifts!

JESUS FACING AN ANNOYING FINANCIAL REQUIREMENT

I stumbled upon a passage last year that still causes me to scratch my head and wonder. The passage is Matthew 17:24-27: "When they came to Capernaum, those who collected the two-drachma tax came to Peter and said, 'Does your teacher not pay the two-drachma tax?' He said, 'Yes.' And when he came into the house, Jesus spoke to him first, saying, 'What do you think, Simon? From whom do the kings of the earth collect customs or poll-tax, from their sons or from strangers?' When Peter said, 'From strangers,' Jesus said to him, 'Then the sons are exempt. However, so that we do not offend them, go to the sea and throw in a hook, and take the first fish that comes up; and when you open its mouth, you will find a shekel. Take that and give it to them for you and Me.'"

Here is Jesus of Nazareth, incarnate Son of the living God. He is healing the sick, raising the dead, cleansing lepers, and doing leadership development with twelve men who will carry on his ministry to the ends of the earth. Amidst this and so much more, all eternally important tasks, he is confronted with the obligation to pay a temple tax. The name itself is hilarious. Temples are made to worship God and he was God! Why in the world should Jesus have to stop what he was doing to attend to such a stupid requirement?

What is remarkable to me is how Jesus responds. He first questions Peter about the mandate, creating a unique learning opportunity for his disciple. Peter expresses the idea that Jesus should not have to abide by this requirement. Jesus agrees with the truth of that interpretation. The tax is something that he should not be subjected to. However, Jesus does not rail against the requirement. He does not go outside and start arguing with people. He does not ignore it or dismiss it with passive-aggressive indifference. He does not allow the unreasonable requirement to shake his self-confidence. He does not give it the power to demean the essence of who he is. Instead, Jesus responds in a remarkable way. He relies upon God, who provides a sovereign and miraculous grace to meet the need. Often we too need extra grace to meet what can seem like insane requirements when we are busy with ministry opportunities that, for all practical purposes, appear to be a much better use of our time and efforts.

In the midst all of this, Jesus of Nazareth says that he is doing it because he does not want to offend them. This is utterly astounding. If we look at Jesus with the Pharisees two chapters earlier (Matthew 15:1-21), we see that he is wholly willing to offend them. He confronts the Pharisees about their hypocrisy and proclaims that they honor God only with their lips yet their hearts are far from God. When his disciples come later and ask Jesus if he realized his statements offended the Pharisees, Jesus criticizes them further. He says, in essence, they are blind guides leading blind men into pits. He uses the instance again as a teaching opportunity for the disciples and then he leaves. Jesus never seems to waste one moment worrying that he might have offended the Pharisees. Yet when it came to a seemingly illegitimate and unreasonable financial requirement, he took steps to keep from offending anyone.

Isn't that remarkable? What does it mean for those of us in cross-cultural ministry partnerships? Does it mean that there are many things in life worthy of confronting and arguing about, like those issues that Jesus confronted in the Pharisees, but when it comes to money issues he wants us to get along? Does it mean that these are not the places worthy of conflict and anger? Does it mean that we should take all the steps necessary to be sure we do not offend each other when it comes to financial issues? Is it a prelude to Paul's exhortation in Romans 13 that these annoying financial requirements are often the result of governing authorities, and there is no authority except from God, so we should honor them? I cannot say that I have the answers to these questions, but I find God's actions in these earlier passages and Jesus' behavior to be quite compelling.

Don't You Trust Me?

The hardest question I have faced when I talk about financial accountability or when I seek to implement some form of internal financial control is this penetrating query: "But won't people think you do not trust them?" Or it might be a direct question from the person on the other side of the accountability process: "Why do you have to count the cash box or examine receipts? Don't you trust me?" The question ratchets up in intensity when it is an indigenous partner and the context is a culture where colonialism has been rampant. For many in ministry, there is a belief that you can either have good financial accountability or good cross-cultural relationships, but not both. However, is that what Scripture teaches us? Is it truly a seesaw whereby one of these areas always suffers whenever there is a gain in the other?

This specific query triggers in me all kinds of internal questions. What is trust? Does trust mean a lack of accountability? Does financial accountability mean we cannot have happy and flourishing relationships?

Do We Need Financial Accountability?

It would be nice to live in a world where no one ever sinned and people always did what was right in the sight of God. However, for the time being we are still on earth and weird things happen. For this reason, we need to think carefully about how we can contextualize accountability processes so they work in many diverse settings.

CONTEXTUALIZING ACCOUNTING PROCESSES

For years executives have assumed they could export their current business models around the globe. That assumption has to change.

—C. K. PRAHALAD AND KENNETH LIEBERTHAL,
"THE END OF CORPORATE IMPERIALISM"

A friend of mine was born and raised in Africa. When he was in his late teens, a civil war erupted. Catastrophic events unfolded, his home was burned to the ground, and many were slaughtered with senseless cruelty. He fled to another region of the continent because leaders of the new regime were trying to force him to fight on their behalf. He remained in another country, studied diligently until the war subsided and later returned to his homeland to begin rebuilding.

Once at home, he became involved in a number of community development initiatives to try to bring some sense of hope after such a horrific period in the nation's history. However, it was then he began to realize that many within his country were conning Westerners to get funding to help victims of violence, only to use the designated funding to amass personal fortunes. As he learned of these elaborate cons, he decided to search the web and see if any funding was being given to his village which was not making it to those truly in need. As he searched he found a site that showed an elaborate hospital that was being built. It had many rooms to treat people, state-of-the-art medical equipment, even new ambulances that would be able to reach remote villages. My friend looked at the address where all the pictures were being taken, and he decided to visit. He told me, "Mary, there was not even a chicken coop built on that site! Not even a chicken coop!" He continued to search the web and he found the African leader's name in charge of this project. He tracked down his personal residence in the capital city and saw that it was a sprawling mansion.

The story could have ended there but my friend did something that I thought was quite shrewd. Through the website he was able to locate the Western donor who was providing most of the funding for this venture. Since the donor lived in America, he asked if she would ever like to come to his country and visit a number of community development and rebuilding initiatives. She replied, "Why, yes! That would be wonderful! In fact, I do have a heart for all that has happened in your country."

So my friend helped to coordinate the trip and took this woman to a number of fantastic projects that were changing and impacting many lives. There were rebuilding initiatives, schooling initiatives, job creation initiatives, rehabilitation of child soldiers, and so forth. The scope of what was happening through a number of strategic partnerships in the region was truly spectacular. After touring all of this the woman said, "You know, I support a hospital in this area. Would it be possible to see it? I have tried to make contact with the liaison I have been working with but I have not been able to reach him." My friend said, "Sure, what is the address?" She told him the location and they went together to see the hospital. However, there was nothing—not even a chicken coop! The woman said, "This cannot be right! Are you sure this is the location?" My friend confirmed that it was indeed the location.

What transpired next was a bit unpleasant. The woman began yelling at my friend saying, "You Africans! You cannot be trusted! You are all liars! I sent over $150,000 to fund a hospital and there is nothing here!" My friend replied, "Do not say *all* Africans. You were dealing with a thief. You were dealing with someone with no integrity. You have seen through your visit how much good is being done here and how much integrity there is. It is not my fault that you chose to partner with someone of poor character. I invited you to come so you could see the difference, and so you would not continue giving to a thief."

The amazing thing from this story is that the financial donor had done everything that, in her context, would have ensured fiscal integrity. The con artist had used his government's letterhead for all of the correspondence, though it is likely that he had a family member working in a government facility who stole this for him. The con artist had provided detailed receipts for every purchase and everything had an impeccable audit trail. There was also a set of fully audited financial statements, detailed photos from each stage of the hospital building project, photos of the recently acquired ambulances, glowing written references, and of course the meticulously updated website so the donor could track it all at a distance. Where did this donor go wrong?

TRADITIONAL PROCESSES MIGHT NOT WORK IN OTHER CONTEXTS

Often we assume that if our processes at home ensure good financial accountability and fiscal integrity, they will have the same result in other cultural contexts.[1] However, this assumption is wholly inaccurate in many parts of the world. For example, in many countries receipts mean absolutely nothing. If you ask for a receipt the merchant will ask, "How much do you want me to make it out for?" In many schemes, two people work in conjunction so a larger receipt is issued and the person making the purchase on behalf of an employer or mission agency splits the difference with the seller. Audited financial statements are only reputable if auditors cannot be easily bribed or coerced by family members to publish inaccurate statements or to look the other direction when impropriety is present.

In this instance, the pictures were an accurate reflection of a hospital in its various stages of growth. The problem was the pictures were of a different hospital being built in a different village by a different organization! The scam artist in this situation was great at producing timely financial statements and timely reporting. In fact, the woman was overjoyed that she had found an African who was punctual and careful to provide all she needed and requested. The harsh reality, however, was that the entire thing was a lie.

Accountability Processes Need to Be Contextualized

To blindly export processes without first examining the context is foolish. We cannot expect the processes that work in our own cultural context to have the same meanings or outcomes in another. Frequently, if Majority World partners are hesitant to implement our requests, it is because the processes are not even rational in their cultural context. A little care in the initial research stage before a new partnership is established can alleviate enormous amounts of frustration for all partners involved!

What is reasonable for the context? Sometimes we have processes that inherently "assume" a high level of accounting skill and knowledge will be located on the field. However, this might not be the case, and it might not even be necessary. What is the accounting knowledge of the people who will be receiving funds? Are there many college-educated people, or is it an agrarian community? What type of accounting software, if any, is commonplace in the area? What are other ministries working in that context doing to help ensure fiscal integrity? It is important to assess this early so when the partnership begins and funds are sent, there are no surprises. Often we can dial back the reporting expectations on the field and do the more detailed write-ups and reporting from a home office. Expectations need to be based in reality and they need to be tailored in a way so they do not create an unnecessary burden for field staff. Poorly designed accountability processes can cause Majority World partners to get bogged down to such an extent it actually begins to hinder the contribution they can make to the kingdom.

Let's pretend that there is a Western partner, and he or she wants financial reports on a set date, say fifteen days after the end of each quarter. However, the field has never been able to close its books that quickly. Utility bills and other key pieces of information they need to account accurately for their quarterly expenditures do not even start to arrive until twenty-five days after the close of each month. If the outside donor is not aware of this, he or she will grow angry and frustrated by delays, and the field staff will resent the unreasonable demands. Better to find out these details early and craft expectations that are reasonable and can truly be met. Then you are not setting yourself up for unnecessary and potentially destructive conflict later.

Separate liaison and audit functions. Over the years I have come to believe that having a close personal relationship is one of the most important things to ensure fiscal integrity. One of the best ways to foster this is to separate out the compliance function from the support role or liaison function. What does this mean? It means there needs to be a person who takes the time to form a level of warmth, care and trust with the financial staff on the other end of the partnership. This person creates a feeling of safety, and people can admit if they are having a problem or are unsure how to handle a given situation. Having this level of rapport is truly priceless, as things can be dealt with early when a problem is still small. Otherwise, it remains hidden and grows.

When I first began working with Wycliffe International, I was in this type of role. I formed friendships with people in numerous countries where we worked. I came alongside people. I wanted to help and support them in their work. I communicated that there were no "dumb" questions, and they never needed to feel embarrassed to ask anything. I made sure I promptly answered their questions and addressed their concerns. Problems were dealt with quickly and things went exceedingly well. Years later, after marrying and settling in the States, I was asked to serve as the international audit coordinator. People who were always open and uncensored around me began to weigh each word carefully. This is because compliance functions, by and large, do not engender trust and openness. However, ministries need both support *and* compliance functions to ensure the highest levels of fiscal integrity. If you try to merge the same person into both roles, it will only do a disservice to both.

Internet communication. One of the most helpful things about the incredible growth of technology is the ability to communicate more meaningfully, and at a much cheaper price, with people all around the world. If the only way you communicate is through written reports, you will not know the full scope of what is happening. However, there are many ways to talk with partners in other countries through the Internet. There are webcams and video conferencing software so you can see one another, making it possible to catch the subtle cues of facial expressions and voice tones. It is easy to make standing meetings or appointments and even talk weekly, sharing professional concerns as well as personal concerns and prayer requests. If indigenous partners do not have the capacity to fund these tools, it is wise for wealthier partners to purchase this equipment. It facilitates longevity in relationships and provides a way to deal with issues and concerns quickly and in a much more personable manner.

Personal visits. In the hospital story we see that one personal visit early on might have led to a totally different outcome. Personal visits can go far in developing genuine care and trust in cross-cultural partnerships. However, visits alone cannot wholly ensure fiscal integrity as we discovered in the chapter about status. Adding personal visits in conjunction with some of the other points we have mentioned will help to ensure a higher level of fiscal integrity in ministry partnerships.

Understand the role of audits. Many Western funding agencies require that an outside audit be conducted when funds are sent abroad. They put a great emphasis on this external audit report because, in their own home context, the audit profession is credible. Nonetheless, as seen with companies like Enron, even in the United States auditors can at times be bought at a price to issue unreliable reports. It is important to know if audits in the country where you are partnering are credible. If so, it is more respectful to have an audit firm within the country handle the audit engagement. Then it becomes, for instance, an Indian auditing an Indian or a Kenyan auditing another Kenyan. As a whole this is a much healthier precedent. The key is being sure that the external audit firm is reliable and the people conducting the audit are in no way related to the person or organization being audited.

Triangulate for validation. We have examined how collective cultures function and the implication of indirect versus direct communication styles. In the West we often like direct communication styles, and we bristle at having a backdoor avenue for getting at the truth. We want "all the cards on the table," and we want everything to be upfront. However, in many cultures the best way to ensure good fiscal integrity is to form a network of contacts who can verify that the results being portrayed are true. Other missionaries and other indigenous leaders are good sources for this type of information. They can easily confirm if a school was truly built or if a local church is indeed meeting and growing. It is helpful to begin assessing if it is possible to form and build this extended group of contacts as soon as any new cross-cultural partnership is being considered. The more you are able to triangulate, by verifying things through other contacts, the greater confidence you can have that the information you are receiving is genuine.

At times hire your own translator. If audits within the country cannot be relied on and you need to do you own compliance testing, be sure you hire your own translator. Do not let the organization you are auditing provide the translation services. I hope the logic for this is clear. You will not be able to confirm the authenticity of information if a translator is biased. This is important for those visits where fiscal integrity is being examined. It is not at all necessary, however, when you are going for other types of visits. Ideally it is best if both the liaison serving the partnership and any external auditor speak the language themselves. Then it becomes a nonissue.

A CAUTIONARY WORD ABOUT BUDGETS

Arguments and misunderstandings about budgets have been pervasive in the missions community and have spanned so many continents that I want to take a few moments to address this issue explicitly. In many countries there are people who feel financial integrity cannot exist unless a ministry is working from a pre-

determined and preapproved budget. However, this is not necessarily the case. Much of the world does not work from budgets. A
budget assumes a level of normalcy and a reliable infrastructure
whereby people can actually plan ahead and assume those plans
are likely to occur. When I have traveled to some parts of the
world, for my own personal life I do not have just plan A, plan B
and plan C. I likely also have plan D, E, F and G. I am by nature a
planner. However, life is so unpredictable in many parts of the
world, it becomes almost impossible to plan. Had I grown up in
those contexts, I would have given up on planning all together as
things were simply too unpredictable.

How do people work in these contexts? When money is available, they spend it on worthy ministry objectives. When money is
not present, they cut back. They often do not spend foolishly. But
they do not budget, because to try to do so in their environment is
often deemed to be not only a bit illogical but truly crazy.

Budgets are one type of fiduciary control that organizations can
use to better ensure that they can reach their goals and that funds
will be spent judiciously. However, budgets in our own context at
times constrain organizations and work against better outcomes.
It is commonplace in government offices that people will frequently buy things they do not need because if they do not spend
their budget this year it might be cut back next year. And no one
wants to be overseeing a shrinking budget! That makes us feel
unsuccessful. Yet if we truly just bought what we needed, fiscally
we would be in much better shape.

Vic, a cross-cultural partner in a church planting ministry, told
me a funny story recently. He was the point person overseeing a
nonprofit organization that raises funds to encourage ministry in
a country in Eastern Europe. He said for ten years he would go
each winter and meet with the staff and teach them and train them
how to write and follow budgets. Vic said it was excruciating be-

cause no matter how carefully he explained the concept, they did not seem to get it. After a decade he wrote to the director to again arrange his visit and he said, "We need to set some time aside to prepare a budget."

This director who he had been coaching for ten years said, "A budget? Why do we need that? I don't know how to write one?" Vic said, "I realized at that moment—stop! It isn't working! They don't understand it. Try it for a while without a budget!"

I said, "So, what happened?" Vic just sat there and laughed and shook his head. He said, "It has been great! From everything I see and everything I hear, no money is being misappropriated. People are coming to Christ. Believers are being discipled. The churches are growing. When they have money, they spend it on good things. When crises arise, they use funds in a way that fosters greater ministry opportunities in the midst of that crisis. And I'm not frustrated all the time!" I just started laughing. What a story! I highlight it to raise the issue that the absence of a budget does not automatically indicate that there is poor stewardship or inappropriate spending.

Two Important Realities in Our World

We face in this new era two distinct realities in our global environment. Amidst all the ministry opportunities that are available to see the kingdom of God advance and the message of Christ reach more people than ever before, there are an unprecedented number of ways to commit fraud. I do not think this should deter us, or even make us skeptical about the world. Jesus said two centuries ago, "Behold, I send you out as sheep in the midst the wolves; so be shrewd as serpents and innocent as doves" (Matthew 10:16). My heart is strengthened and encouraged by that passage. We are able to be innocent and believe that people will do great things in

Christ's name without having to be naive to the realities of our world. Christ urged his disciples to walk in the tension of that statement. The mantle is no more burdensome for us in our time. Human nature has not changed.[2]

Another reality we face is summed up well by Dale Berkey in the book titled *The Disappearing Donor.* He outlines the results of an extensive survey done to better understand why donors stop giving to ministry projects and initiatives. He writes, "The study itself, conducted with the cooperation and assistance of nearly a dozen of the ministries we serve, ended up being about three times as big as the typical Gallup poll."[3] Berkey notes, "The study shows that donors value integrity—honesty and sound business prac- tices—most highly. More than 80% of all donors, lapsed and ac- tive alike, named 'being honest in their business practices' as the quality which, if unfulfilled, would cause them to stop giving. . . . About three-quarters of all donors named 'using your gift only for what they say they will'"[4] as being critical for future giving.

If we want to be able to keep raising funds from people in the West to see the work of God's kingdom advance in the world, we have to find ways to work together that acknowledge this reality. This is the pressure our Western partners are facing in their home contexts. If Christian leaders cannot meet these expectations, they will be unable to rally the financial resources needed to make a substantial difference in this next era of global missions. For this reason, taking time on the front-end to contextualize and form processes to ensure fiscal integrity and accountability will go a long way in helping to ensure the longevity and sustainability of any cross-cultural ministry partnership.

BUT ACCOUNTABILITY IS SO NEGATIVE!

For many cross-cultural partners, it is hard to know how to implement accountability structures and still model values such as dignity and mutuality. Perhaps this tension would not even be present if accountability processes always went both ways and were more holistically integrated throughout all of our work and ministry processes. In Christian ministry we often model worldly processes so that those with less power and resources are accountable to those with greater wealth and power. If we want to truly begin to foster dignity and mutuality, we need to gain greater sensitivity to the power dynamics in our partnerships. The next chapter will begin to address this issue.

Fostering Dignity and Mutuality

You are too powerful to be good partners." So the charge came from an Anglican bishop in Tanzania. John Watters was serving as the Africa Area Director for Wycliffe Bible Translators International. The setting was a conference where indigenous partners were discussing how the ministry of Bible translation and literacy might advance throughout the continent. As he explains, "It was a moment of truth telling. These times are usually uncomfortable but necessary. They clarify the current issues inherent in the process of working together. They usually come in the form of one or two sentences that cut to the core of an issue. In these cases they have to do with issues of power, relationships, and equity."[1] John explains that the bishop who made this comment is still a friend and partner in ministry.

The statement caught John off-guard. He asked this leader, "So how is it that we are 'too powerful to be good partners'?" John writes,

> The bishop explained. Those of us from the West come with economic, educational and organizational strength that cannot be matched locally. There is no way local partners can be equal in those areas. He was not saying we could not be part-

ners; just that it would take a lot of hard work for us to be good partners. Part of that hard work would be to recognize and fully appreciate the strengths that the non-Western partner brought to the partnership. As he noted, with our strengths we could pursue almost anything we wanted without regard for others. But would such an attitude or unilateral action achieve what we really wanted to achieve? It was highly unlikely. Such attitudes and actions do not build capacity in the local church or community. They do not lead to sustainable programs. So partnership was going to take great effort on our part to make it succeed. Partnership was not usually going to come "naturally." It would require great wisdom from God and an abundance of the fruit of the Spirit.[2]

This discussion between John Watters and his African partner intersects well with the concern about mutuality in cross-cultural partnerships. All too often if we come from wealth or a cultural heritage of privilege, we do not value or notice the wisdom and resources of those coming from a less affluent heritage. This is a frequent dynamic around the world in business settings, in ministries and even between individuals within a church. For whatever reason, it seems to be a common and prevalent blind spot as affluence increases. I am not sure that partnering well comes naturally to any person of means. I believe it is possible for us to grow and become good cross-cultural ministry partners, but it will take intentional effort and a regular dose of heartfelt humility. My hope is that this section will shed light on the realities of these power issues and how they can be navigated so our ministry partnerships will truly model dignity and mutuality.

What About Jesus?

Jesus is the ultimate high-powered and highly resourced partner in global missions. Colossians 1:15-17 says, "He is the image of the invisible God, the firstborn of all creation. For by Him all things were created, both in the heavens and on earth, visible and invisible, whether thrones or dominions or rulers or authorities—all things have been created by Him and for Him. He is before all things, and in Him all things hold together." I am glad Jesus didn't say, "You know, there is such a big gap between what I can do and what you can do. Why don't we just work separately?" If he had said that, we would all understand. Yet Jesus does the opposite. He works with us and through us and in us. We will examine how he does this in the final chapter. However, I believe if we keep our eyes and hearts fixed on him as Hebrews 12:2 admonishes us to do, we can transform into his image and we can be a blessing in cross-cultural partnerships.

HOW GOD SEES PEOPLE

At the heart of this issue of dignity and mutuality is how we perceive ourselves and how we perceive others. Or, perhaps more accurately stated, at the heart of the issue is whether we perceive others as God does. God's love is the same for all of his children. One culture or group of people is not higher in God's heart and in his mind than another. One is not more valued than the other. Innate in Christian doctrine is the concept of *imago Dei*. We are all made in the image and likeness of God. We see this from the earliest passage of Scripture: "Let Us make man in Our image, according to Our likeness . . ." (Genesis 1:26).

For reasons we will never wholly absorb, probably because it is so deeply steeped in the very essence of divine love, God aligns himself with us. God places his image in our created beings and he takes it as a personal affront if we treat any human being in a demeaning or hurtful way. Lest there be any confusion about this

Jesus was quite clear in Matthew 25:40 when he said, "Truly I say to you, to the extent that you did it to one of these brothers of Mine, even the least of them, you did it to Me."

WHAT ACTIONS OR PROCESSES MIGHT HELP?

In global missions there is a history of paternalistic behavior steeped in a false sense of superiority. This has taken place alongside a history of colonialism. Along the way many have been hurt, sometimes quite unintentionally, despite good intentions and a desire to do the will of God. Is there a way to change this? Are there any steps we can take to begin to turn the tide, so to speak? When I consider these questions, four things come to mind.

Greatly value all resources, not just money. Daniel Rickett says, "Partners who collaborate primarily out of benevolence run the risk of overvaluing their contribution and under-valuing the partner's contribution. When that happens, the overrated partner can easily fall into the trap of paternalism. To prevent this, partners should identify the reasons they are equally committed to the partnership, put it in writing, and revisit those reasons as the partnership evolves."[3]

I spoke to some African colleagues in my Ph.D. program a few years back and explained that I wanted to research how to foster better cross-cultural relationships in environments that also fostered high standards of accountability. One said,

> Mary—why do you Americans act like because you are providing the money, you are bringing the most valuable thing and you should be able to call all the shots? Look at me! Say I am willing to take my family and endure the dangers and the hardships of living in a slum in Nairobi so people can come to Christ. My family is in danger. My health is in danger. Daily I work exceedingly long hours. But my body has a

natural resistance to malaria so I am better equipped than you to serve in that place. I also know the language and the culture, so I can experience fruitful outcomes in ministry more quickly. Why, in light of all these contributions, is money viewed as the most valuable resource? I think the person putting their life and the lives of their family members on the line should be valued equally if not more!

What do you say to such a question? To me these questions and concerns are wholly legitimate. Why do wealthy cultures almost instinctively believe and act as though their contribution is the most valuable? I think it goes back to messages we heard when we were children. Stan Nussbaum explains this reality in the United States when he says, "Since many Americans do not deal with their own cultural baggage, the people around them are forced to deal with it."[4] Part of that baggage is deeply ingrained in us through the cultural proverbs and sayings that we heard growing up. A phrase as simple as "money talks" becomes an assumed reality. Another is, "He who pays the piper calls the tune." There is even the deformed twist of the golden rule that many see playing out as a daily reality in all facets of society: "He who has the gold makes the rules." If we do not step back and critically analyze our inherited belief systems, we will make some serious mistakes. And it is not just those in the United States who are prone to such arrogance. Over the years I have seen wealthy Christian donors in virtually every country of the world run the same risk if they are not careful. For in most nations in the world, financial resources seem to determine who gets to call the shots.

In his book, John Rowell describes a healthier way of partnering. He says, "In our covenant relationship, paternalism has no place. We walk as brothers and sisters, coequal children of one heavenly Father, serving a mutually agreed-upon agenda. No special deference is due westerners because of our relative wealth. Bosnians are generally viewed as wiser than us in understanding their own culture and in strategizing how to reach it."[5]

Choosing to value and bring to the forefront all the sacrifices and resources being made available to fulfill a ministry goal or vision is essential. Only when everything is on the table can money be seen for what it is, simply one of the many resources God provides for his children to accomplish his work in the world.

Develop accountability that goes in all directions. In the book *African Friends and Money Matters*, David Maranz does a superb job comparing and contrasting the Western versus African worldview regarding money.[6] Often these differences are misunderstood and many remain unaware of their roots. Maranz writes, "Colonialism left another legacy. During the colonial period African leaders were not accountable to the people under them, but to their colonial masters. These in turn were accountable only to their home governments. The local people were there to be controlled, not informed. Surely this colonial pattern left indelible marks across the continent."[7] One of the biggest difficulties about financial accountability is this issue. Because the missionaries appear to be "unaccountable," at least as far as the Africans can see, it seems unfair and discriminatory for Africans to now have to give account for funds they use in ministry. However, the missionaries were accountable, but not to the people in the context where they were serving.

I believe accountability is inherently a part of healthy Christianity. Accountability reminds all of us that God is watching, he is taking note, and in the day of judgment we will all have to give an account for everything we did, everything we said and every decision we made about how we used resources. Nothing will be hidden. All will be out in the open. Accountability is what God designed to enable us to learn from one another, coach each other and grow into maturity in Christ. That is why the research in emotional intelligence is so intriguing. It holds many parallels to training in the growth of cultural intelligence. Without realizing it Daniel Goleman proved through his research that accountability is necessary for any lasting personal growth as well as for maximum effectiveness in the workplace.[8]

The problem is not that financial accountability is discriminatory to cross-cultural partners or that it is, in and of itself, inherently paternalistic. The greater issue is that we need to begin to redeem the essence of the meaning of true accountability and implement it throughout all processes and parts of our ministries. It should not just be the people receiving funds who are held accountable. If that is the case, it is hard to not make the case that financial accountability is discriminatory and paternalistic.

Top leaders in our organizations need to be accountable not only to their boards but to everyone within their organizations. As Mathew 25:40 indicates, we will be held accountable for how we treat everyone, even the "least of these" (NRSV). People donating time need to be accountable. No person giving any resource to the partnership should be unaccountable. Thought and care needs to be invested at the outset to determine how healthy and godly accountability might look if it truly went both ways and was integrated into all aspects of cross-cultural ministry. If everyone is accountable to one another, there will no longer be the feeling that one group is being singled out for discrimination. As God's sons and daughters, in the end he will hold us all accountable, and we are doing no one any favors by developing processes that reflect a different reality.

Destroy any remnant of a culture of silence. When paternalism is in place, there is a directional limitation on how communication can flow. In a family, the father is the head of the home. He is supposed to have the last and final word. If children disagree, they are to be quiet, stop complaining and fall in line with his authority and direction. In ministries with paternalistic environments, a culture of silence prevails. If the "paternal" figure has a concern, it is expressed and promptly addressed. The thoughts and opinions of others are never able to be fully expressed. Often if they do risk expressing them, they are never taken seriously. If a culture of silence is not crushed, the full scope of information and insight we need to make truly good decisions lies dormant. As a result, ministries are far less effective than they could be.

David Bohm was a renowned physicist and theorist. Later in his life he focused much of his time and thinking on human communication and dialogue. He wrote of "blocks," or hindrances, to dialogue. He said, "The very nature of such a 'block', is, however, that it is a kind of insensitivity or anesthesia about one's own contradictions."[9] If we are not wholly committed to drawing all people into dialogue so any genuine concerns are able to be addressed, we will remain anesthetized to our own unhealthy behaviors, and we will hinder the advancement of the kingdom of God.

Forgive and remember so lasting change can take place. It would be nice if all we had to do was say "I will change" and bad habits evaporated instantaneously into thin air. However, that is not the reality of life, and emotional intelligence research affirms this.[10] It takes time to change, especially if some habits are deeply ingrained. I have struggled over the years with the role of forgiveness in lasting change and transformation. At times I have had people say, "Oh, I am so sorry. Do you forgive me?" I would say, "Yes. I forgive you." Then, a week or a month later they would do the same thing again. When I would mention that they did it again, as they had in the past, I would be scolded as being "unforgiving for bringing up the past." However, the only reason I remembered the past was because they were doing it again!

It is almost comical to think about it now, but this response really threw me. I believe it is wrong to say I forgive a person, and then keep bringing it up over and over again when the person truly repented and changed. To do so seems emotionally and spiritually abusive. A book was written by a group of people doing peace and reconciliation work in some of the most difficult areas in the world.[11] Seeing forgiveness and reconciliation on a macro level clarified this for me. John Paul Lederach expresses it concisely when he writes, "The challenge of reconciliation is not how to create the place where one can 'forgive and forget.' It is about the far more challenging adventure into the space where individuals and whole communities can remember and change."[12] Anthony Da Silva writes, "Traditionally, forgiveness has tended to be associated with forgetting. Hence the familiar adage 'forgive and forget.' But now having witnessed and heard countless forgiveness stories from South Africa to Latin America, 'forgive and remember' seems like a wiser safeguard; it ensures that we remain alert to not repeating similar painful and unjust actions in the future. Memory makes the past available to us so that we can work through events and traumas without trivializing or denying them."[13]

An Angolan proverb says, "The one who throws the stone forgets; the one who is hit remembers forever."[14] Helmick and Petersen write, "Forgiveness is a word that makes for freedom. . . . Forgiveness makes it possible to remember the past without being held hostage to it. Without forgiveness there is no progress, no linear history, only a return to conflict and cycles of conflict."[15] The International Forgiveness Institute at the University of Wisconsin has done a lot of research on forgiveness.[16] It is fascinating to see this topic through their findings. Forgiveness is a gift we give to ourselves. It makes it impossible for past hurts to keep hurting and injuring us.

Although these authors are dealing with horrific global conflicts like ethnic cleansing and the outcomes of barbarous civil wars, these principles are quite helpful for those working through issues of paternalism in mission contexts. We need to forgive, for our own spiritual health and for the health of others. But as we forgive, both sides need to be committed to remember, to listening to others and to expressing concern if a former bad habit rears its ugly head. We will not change if that concern is silenced. We also need to be willing to set aside the dogma of old meanings as the automatic interpretation for all current behaviors. We need to care enough about the kingdom and about one another to get to the heart and the true reasons behind requests for financial accountability. If we will make that commitment, even annoying financial requirements can become pathways for continued personal growth and spiritual maturity.

ACCOUNTABILITY IS POWERFUL

How we choose to hold one another accountable in our partnerships will tell more about our values than anything else. We can model processes that foster dignity and mutuality. We can also form processes that build capacity and sustainability. We will examine this in the next chapter.

BUILDING CAPACITY
AND SUSTAINABILITY

Give a man a fish and he will eat for a day.
Teach a man to fish and he will eat for a lifetime.

Many churches and mission agencies misunderstand the purpose of partnership. It is not just giving money or cutting a check. We need to go beyond that to the place where we help cross-cultural partners develop infrastructure and capacity so they are sustainable over the long haul. Each group we partner with should be stronger and better off than they were before we started working together."[1] This advice came from Howie Brant, one of the mission leaders I respect most deeply. He has worked with all his heart to help Majority World partners fulfill their dreams and destinies in global missions. His comment needs to be heeded. If dependency can be a negative outcome from partnering cross-culturally, is it possible to partner and share resources in ways that truly do build capacity and foster sustainability? There are numerous incidents of this happening all around the world. The difference frequently lies in our ability to see potential and believe in others, and our ability to work alongside others with patience and grace.

THE PARABLE OF THE BRIDGE

An African friend relayed a parable he heard recently.[2] There were people living on one side of a vast and treacherous canyon. On the other side were all kinds of wonderful opportunities. There were jobs and chances to obtain more education. There were interesting items at those distant markets and people with much wisdom. However, separating the two groups was a frightening precipice that cascaded into intense rapids which would surely take the life of any unfortunate soul who fell trying to cross. Spanning the precipice was a thin and somewhat rickety bridge.

A missionary came from a distant land and met with the people on the far side of the canyon. He said, "Come, let's go to the other side where you will find the resources you need for your lives and for your community." However, the missionary was a tall and muscular person. He seemed to tower over everyone. A small and timid man walked with him to the bridge but was too afraid to cross. At that point the story split off into three alternate endings, much like some movies we can purchase now.

In the first ending the husky missionary said, "Do not be afraid. I will carry you across the bridge." And faithfully and dutifully he carried the timid man. He continued to carry people across the bridge faithfully, at great sacrifice to himself and to his family. However, after four years he had to return to his homeland for furlough. The people on the distant side of the canyon abruptly stopped making the trip across the ravine and all the progress they had seen as a community vanished within a few months.

In the second ending the husky missionary began carrying the timid man back and forth across the canyon. Soon he began car-

rying others as well. The missionary had the best of intentions;
however, over time he became tired. He explained to the people
that they needed to start walking across themselves. But they re-
sisted so he continued to carry them. One day the strength in his
arms gave way, and he dropped the man he was carrying into the
raging waters. The man's dead body was later found down stream.
The missionary was so saddened and distraught that he went
home and lost all hope that he would ever be able to help the
people on the distant side of the canyon.

In the third ending when the timid man asked to be carried,
the missionary said he could not do it. He explained that if he
carried the timid man, over time he would need to leave, and
then the distant village would be left in a vulnerable place. The
missionary also knew that his own strength was limited and
there was a chance over time that he might drop someone. Instead, he offered something different to the timid man. He said,
"If you are willing to make the journey, I will walk before you
and hold your hand the entire way. If you get scared we will stop
and I will talk you through it. We will take as long as you need.
I will not rush you." The timid man agreed and with great trepi-
dation he began the journey.

That first trek across took a long time! The missionary was patient, however, for he realized the importance of that initial in-
vestment. When the timid man wanted to return home, he again
walked back with the missionary in front, holding his hand. The
return trip, however, was shorter. The next day the timid man
wanted to visit the distant village again. The process continued,
with the missionary going first. This time the trip took only one
third as long as the first trip. This continued until the timid man
was no longer timid and until he no longer needed the missionary's help. The missionary encouraged the man to provide similar
support and guidance to his community and train others to help

lead their people to the place of resources and opportunities. The man answered the call, faithfully and patiently helping others to cross until they too were no longer afraid to make the journey.

The missionary's term came to an end, and he returned home for furlough. However, the village in the distance grew and flourished. People acquired needed medical care. Children gained an education. People came to faith in Christ. Literacy and all kinds of community development projects were undertaken. Infant mortality rates plummeted. The people in the distant village grew and became great leaders in the region and in their nation.

WHAT IT TAKES TO BUILD CAPACITY

I like the parable of the bridge because it highlights how important vision is. If we do not have a vision for the development of capacity in our partnerships, we will hinder the fullness of what God wants to accomplish. In a sad way this parable highlights the mistakes made in missions over the years. It shows with vivid clarity what happens when we begin with the wrong assumptions. Thus, we need to think clearly. If we hope to be in a better place over time, we need reasonable assessments not only of our own strengths and abilities but also of others'. Vision is one of the most powerful concepts in the world. We see in Hebrews 11 that all kinds of men and women have done great things because they could see what was unseen. Vision provides internal capacity to overcome difficulties and entrenched behaviors so we can work differently in the world.[3]

The importance of vision. Bryant Myers talks about how World Vision utilizes appreciative inquiry as one method for getting at the potential and strengths of a community.[4] Appreciative inquiry is different from many research methodologies.[5] It focuses on the positive things that are happening in an organization or culture. It asks about stories that have been life-giving. It looks for themes in the stories and begins to discern areas for future inquiry. It then works with people to create shared images of what the future might look like. Last, it finds ways to help create that future.[6] Myers writes,

> World Vision Tanzania has been very creative in adapting and using the appreciative approach. Typically, a community welcomes a development NGO with hospitality and presents it with a list of things the community would like done. . . . Insisting on a discussion focusing on what has worked and on when and how the community has been successful in the past is very helpful in getting past the initial view of the NGO as the giver of good things. Through community meetings and focus groups, World Vision Tanzania works with the community using an appreciative framework to hear the community's answers to questions. . . .
>
> The net result of such an inquiry is often spectacular. The laundry list of problems the community would like the NGO to fix is lost in the enthusiasm of describing what is already working. The community comes to view its past and itself in a new light. We do know things. We do have resources. We have a lot to be proud of. We are already on a journey. God has been good to us. We can do something. We are not godforsaken. This is a major step toward recovering the community's true identity and discovering its true vocation. With these discoveries a major transformational frontier has been crossed.[7]

Glenn Schwartz frequently tells a story about a congregation in South Africa. The threshold that needed to be crossed was obedience on the part of the pastor but also vision to begin to see church members as God saw them. Glenn writes,

In South Africa there is a church called the Assemblies of God. Every year one of their senior ministers by the name of Rev. Nicholas Bhengu went to North America to raise money for his church. Once while he was in North America God spoke to him and said, "Go back home and get the money from your own people." Rev. Bhengu replied, "But, Lord, how can I do that? The only people in my church are women and children; the women are unemployed and the men don't come. How am I supposed to get the money from them?"

God spoke to Rev. Bhengu very directly and said these four things:

1. Go home and teach the women how to care for their families.

2. Teach them how to bring their husbands to the Lord.

3. Teach them how to make something with their hands so they can earn a living.

4. Teach them to give some of it back to God in thanksgiving—in other words, to tithe.

That is not the end of the story. Every year the people from this denomination—now whole families—gather for a weekend conference at a place called Thaba Nchu in South Africa. Several years ago they met for that conference and took a collection of nearly four million South African Rand—in one weekend! At the exchange rate at the time, that was nearly one million U.S. dollars in one collection. It was from the same church that at one time was comprised of unemployed women and children![8]

Before we jump into missions work, are we willing to take time to see people in new ways? Are we willing to help them see their own abilities, capacities and strengths? Are we coming to rescue, or are we coming to empower? Innate in all of us is a desire to be needed. However, if we work from that motivation or ethos, any short-term gains in the partnership will likely be overshadowed by long-term dependency.

The importance of grace and patience. One of the things I appreciate most about Scripture is that it does not gloss over difficult realities of life. I especially love Jesus and how he interacted with people during his time on earth. I am amazed at his honesty and humanity, especially when it came to training his future "leadership team." Matthew 17:14-23 is one of those passages. Jesus had sent his disciples into the world on various excursions already. He knew his time with them was soon coming to an end. Yet a heartsick and distraught father came and fell on his knees before Christ in utter despair. What was the father's request? "Lord, have mercy on my son, for he is a lunatic and is very ill; for he often falls into the fire and often in the water. I brought him to Your disciples, and they could not cure him" (Matthew 17:15-16). How does Jesus respond? Is he neutral? Did Jesus say, "That's OK, disciples, just bring him to me. I'll take care of it." No. Instead he responds, "You unbelieving and perverted generation, how long shall I be with you? How long shall I put up with you? Bring him here to Me" (Matthew 17:17).

It should give us hope to know that Jesus also appeared at times to get frustrated with his disciples in the midst of the leadership development process. He was occasionally annoyed by their lack of faith. He was annoyed at their pettiness. When cloaked with humanity, I think God simply got tired of dealing with humans at times. We see that in him and we see that quality in ourselves as we train and retrain others over and over again. And yet it is important to recognize what Jesus did not do. He never said, "OK, I am done with you. I am going to take it over from here. I am going to change the plan, live here on earth permanently and run this ministry myself. I know I can obviously do a better job than these twelve. For heaven's sake, they don't even have faith to heal this boy. If you want a job done right, you've got to just do it yourself! Enough with this capacity-building stuff!" Amidst Jesus' frustration with his disciples, Jesus never gave up on them. Amidst his frustration with us, Jesus never gives up on us. He saw what the disciples would someday become and he sees what we will one day become. For this reason Jesus keeps investing in us. For this reason he perseveres and is long-suffering when it comes to the process of building capacity.

BUILDING CAPACITY IN THE FINANCE AREA

When it comes to missions and the area of money in cross-cultural ministry partnerships, there are specific steps we can take to help build capacity and sustainability. For any church or nonprofit organization, there has to be an ability to receive, account for and distribute funds effectively. If any of these areas are insufficiently developed, there will be negative ripple effects on the entire ministry. Here are some ideas that have worked well in various parts of the world. The key, however, is to use them as points for dialogue with your partners and not as an automatic "cut and paste" for your ministry. They should be launching pads to begin addressing specific needs. However, how that need is met must be contextualized in each culture so it is relevant and sustainable over the long haul.

Developing financial policies. Some foundations require that indigenous organizations have stated financial policies in order to apply for and receive funding for various ministries. It is common for a Western partner to be a bridge connecting these types of resources with indigenous partners. However, a virtual standstill can occur when the Western partner asks an indigenous partner for their "financial policy document" to pass on to the

foundation or outside funder. Like a deer caught in the head-
lights of an automobile, it is not uncommon for an indigenous
partner to be stopped in his or her tracks by such a statement.
What does it mean? What do they want? It would take us years
to develop something like that.

I always think of a corollary in my personal life. In the midst of
remodeling projects, I have had people say, "Well, just change all
your outlets. It isn't hard." I just stare at them. When I look at outlets I see electrical power that has the capacity to kill me. I do not
know how to change electrical outlets. I just stare at them, and
they stare at me. I think they are nuts, and they think I am stupid.
And what transpires as a result? Absolute no progress is made.
Years pass and still I have never changed the electrical outlets.

I have a friend who needed new outlets in her house. Her dad
came to visit from out of town for a day. He took about an hour
and talked her through a simple book that taught her about electricity and outlets. He then showed her how to turn off her power.
Next he changed an outlet and let her watch. He then carefully
walked her through the steps to change another outlet. He then
had her change a couple of outlets and he watched. After his short
visit, he went home and over the next two weeks she changed all
the other outlets in her house. In essence, he first walked her
across the bridge holding her hand. Then he walked beside her.
Then he went home and she could walk across all by herself.

When I think of her accomplishment, I think she is a genius.
She tells me that it isn't hard, but to me, it is still an utter mystery.
Why? Because I am expected to do what appears to me to be a
huge task, and I know nothing about it. I have had no training in
the area, and I have never been given any steps or guidance about
how to get there. And I do not trust that I can just read a book and
do it. Electricity is dangerous, and I want someone to walk me
through it to be sure I do not kill myself.

That example will seem silly to many of you who understand how electricity works and who have changed outlets in your homes. However, when we ask indigenous partners to provide detailed financial policies, the request is frequently a foreign one for them. They do not understand what is needed and they have no idea how to get there. So they stall and make excuses or they evade the subject altogether. A far more helpful approach is for the foreign partner to sit down with indigenous leaders and just ask questions about a number of different issues.

For instance, if money comes in and is earmarked to help sick children, will you spend it for that purpose? Is there any reason you would deviate from spending funds for a purpose that differs from what the donor requested? Under what circumstances would that happen? Do you keep any funds to help when emergencies arise? How do you cover emergencies? If income drops, how do you handle expenses like salaries and rent? Do you ever borrow funds? How do you keep track of that? There are many basic questions you can ask. Listen carefully to each response. Then summarize what you hear by saying, "From this talk it sounds like you would normally do this and this and this, unless a certain exception arises and then you would do that. Is this correct?" If they respond affirmatively, you draft a policy for them based on their responses, and let them review and make changes to it as they see fit. In the end, you will have a good finance policy crafted.

Another easy way to approach it is to provide several different samples or copies of finance policies used by other Christian nonprofit organizations for them to review. They can then decide if any of those represent how they will be doing business. If there are some differences, all that is needed is minor editing. It is likely that for years these partners never needed to have their practices and policies documented, yet often they functioned well. Often the primary reason they need these policies documented now is because they are seeking funds from a partner in a low-context culture.

Training finance people. In the Majority World more and more funds are coming from local and foreign sources for the work of the kingdom. In many countries where they have sought to nationalize mission programs, those who put a great emphasis on integrity and ethics training for treasurers and finance people do the best. If people do not trust that funds they give will get to specific programs or to people in need, they will not give. Many churches have built discipleship programs that spend extensive time looking at Scriptures about money and accountability. By dealing with the core of people's hearts, you can greatly increase the likelihood that the church treasurer and staff will be held in high esteem and will be trusted. When that is in place, the rest falls in line, for then there will be a deep motivation in the hearts of those same people to find the best tools to keep track of the God-given resources under their stewardship.

Creating reporting that is helpful and relevant. I like the comments that Bryant Myers makes on this issue. He writes,

> Whom is the evaluation for? Too often it is for the donor. While accountability to donors is important, the kind of evaluation they seek may not be all that helpful to the community and its learning process. Sometimes, the evaluation is for the development agency, since it desires, quite correctly, to be professional, and professionals test the impact of their work rather than trust in their marketing stories. But the most important audience for continuous learning must be the community. It is the community's development, and anything that takes what is the community's and places it at the service of others mars the community's identity, making it poorer.[9]

As reporting and accountability structures are built, we have to keep in mind that reporting should not be designed to only meet the needs of a foreign financial donor or partner. Accountability and reporting can be designed to truly inform, coach, train and guide those doing the ministry so they can be even more effective. There is no "right way" to implement this. But through dialogue and discussion you can begin to uncover what types of reporting will truly empower all involved in the cross-cultural ministry partnership.

CAPACITY IN REMOTE AREAS

A liaison for a church-planting partnership in Latin America told me this story:

> I was in this really remote area and these indigenous leaders picked me up in a brand new white pickup truck. They took me for a meal and I kept wondering how they were able to purchase such a nice vehicle. Later the story came out that the government was building roads deeper and deeper into the interior. These indigenous mission leaders either had to walk or use a mule to go 25 kilometers or more. Some village leaders were inciting people to keep the evangelicals out of the remote communities. These indigenous missionaries tried to hitchhike into the remote areas but people stopped picking them up. They then decided to get 60 local families to come in together and purchase a truck for the ministry. They told me that the local leaders cannot keep them from traveling on the road any more, and they are able to reach even more communities than ever! The liaison said, "You should have seen what they did to the back of that truck. They installed benches and I think 18 people could ride in the back. It was amazing!"

Do we believe people have the capacity to give to ministry programs, even when they live in remote and what appear to us to be "poor" regions in the world? Dependency is a problem when we do not see correctly and discern correctly. What is a need in one place might not be a need in another. Often there are local resources and ways to solve issues that are far wiser and better than imported solutions. We need to take time to examine these before we begin to import outside funds to do what the community, church or ministry can accomplish on its own. We need to "see" well and be patient if we want to build capacity and see sustainability in partnership endeavors.

We all enter cross-cultural partnerships with the highest of hopes and usually with the best of intentions. We have explored many steps that can be taken to facilitate stronger and healthier cross-cultural partnerships. However, one area continues to catch people off-guard—conflict. We will cover this next.

Part Four

REDEEMING
CONFLICT

CHOOSING YOUR METHOD CAREFULLY

Keith was frustrated with Andrew. Although the partnership started off well, the last several months had been rocky. Andrew seemed to be losing focus. He was spending less of his time on the partnership objectives and, in Keith's mind, too much time preaching in local churches. Keith decided to follow the Matthew 18:15 passage. He flew to Andrew's country and confronted him in person. Andrew did not respond well. He became silent, and in the weeks that followed he seemed to be exhibiting passive-aggressive behavior. Keith was sad about the situation. He thought Andrew was more spiritually mature than that!

Conflict management processes are tools for the practitioner. Depending on the circumstances, the tools we choose have the potential to make things exponentially better or worse. However, few of us realize how much our family and cultural heritage have influenced our perceptions about how conflict should be managed. Sherwood Lingenfelter, a respected cross-cultural educator, explains that we all have a default culture.[1] When we become engaged in conflict, almost without thinking we default into the patterns modeled by our family members or others close to us. Often these are not the healthiest or most effective measures. When this happens, our well-intentioned methods can actually escalate the very conflict we are seeking to resolve.

Frank Dubinskas addresses the cultural roots of discord in *Hidden Conflict in Organizations*:

> Cultural patterns are often invisible to their own members, and it is the very obviousness of culture that sometimes hides from analysis. Culture is largely constituted out of the taken-for-granted, seldom articulated patterns of everyday action and belief. To the parties in an organizational conflict, their own cultural patterns simply constitute the "natural" way to do things. Each group's particular way of working and understanding their work becomes normalized and turned into a sort of common sense backdrop to everyday life.[2]

THE MATTHEW 18:15-17 PASSAGE

For many from individualistic cultures, Matthew 18:15-17 is the backdrop for our thinking. Jesus said, "If your brother sins, go and show him his fault in private; if he listens to you, you have won your brother. But if he does not listen to you, take one or two more with you, so that by the mouth of two or three witnesses every fact may be confirmed. If he refuses to listen to them, tell it to the church; and if he refuses to listen even to the church, let him be to you as a Gentile and a tax collector." In essence, follow a direct communication style. Deal with the issue head-on with words, and if he does not repent, treat him as an unbeliever.

In my own cultural heritage, most evangelicals understand and, at least in theory, value this process Jesus laid out more than two thousand years ago. Although we might not always follow it, we often feel it is a weakness of character if we do not. In general, individualistic cultures tend to use and favor direct methods of communication to resolve conflicts. They like to speak plainly and clearly, get all the issues out on the table and then seek to resolve things in a timely manner. As a whole, much of the rest of the world tends to favor and utilize indirect methods as a way to deal with conflict. If we do not have our perspective widened to the other methods in Scripture available to us when conflict arises, we will be at an extreme disadvantage and our attempts to bring reconciliation will likely make bad situations even worse.

YOU ARE TREATING ME LIKE A CHILD!

I was asked to do some cultural training for a team of short-term missionaries heading to Asia. In the group was a woman born and raised in Korea. As I explained the difference between direct and indirect confrontational styles, she contributed a helpful story. She said, "In America if people want to resolve a conflict, they think the best way is to come directly to your face and discuss it. They say what they didn't like and how they wish things had been handled differently. In Korea, we do not treat adults this way. We only treat children this way. Adults are supposed to be more sophisticated and able to interpret the social clues which indicate that a behavior or outcome is not acceptable."

Have you ever been in a conflict with a person, and then he or she began to treat you like a child? Does it help the situation or make it worse? How do you respond when you feel as though another adult is treating you like a child? Does it bring the best out of you? Does it foster a better relationship with that person? We need to examine and know what the various styles of confrontation and conflict management mean in each unique context.

FACE, FACE, FACE

Stella Ting-Toomey and John Oetzel have done some ground-breaking research about the meaning of conflict-resolution styles. They explain, "Conflict is a face-threatening process."[3] Because of this, it is important to find ways to resolve conflict so it will not only save face, but will also build face.[4] "Members of individualistic cultures tend to use face-work behaviors that are low-context and direct, emphasize self-face, and reflect individual conflict goals. Members of collectivistic cultures tend to employ facework behaviors that are high-context and indirect, support the other's face, and preserve relational and network harmony."[5]

SOMETIMES I HAVE BEEN ASKED TO "HELP"

At times I have been asked by indigenous organizations to help them with a problem regarding financial accountability. When they meet with me, they are often direct in telling me their fears or concerns about a weakness in their system, a person who seems to be disregarding financial controls and a fear there might be theft, or at least a great vulnerability for it to occur. They often conclude by asking, "Would you be willing to sit in on our elders meeting or our board meeting? Please do not ever mention this person or this situation. Instead, when we ask would you share about what best practices are for other ministries?" I agree, I attend the meetings, and no direct comment is ever raised with the person in question. Instead, I share best practices I have seen in various nonprofit ministries, the sorrow that happens in relationships if theft occurs and the dishonor brought to the name of Christ and the ministry if it occurs. I explain that the "heart" behind good financial controls is to protect people and the ministry, not to be miserly or obsessive or to value money over people. Quite the contrary, I explain that good controls can foster unity and truly wonderful outcomes and deepen trust in others.

Each time I am then thanked for sharing this perspective with the team. It is one of many agenda items. Sometimes afterward the leaders talk about what this might mean for their ministries, and I sit and listen. Often weeks or months later, the original person comes back and says that the situation is resolved and no one felt singled out or lost face. This extremely indirect approach might not be the way to handle a situation where there is known theft or proven impropriety. However, it can help substantially in the early phases when leaders first sense vulnerability in this area.

THIRD-PARTY MEDIATORS

In many individualistic cultures, third-party mediation is normally only used as the very last resort in cases such as bankruptcy, custody battles and divorce settlements. Only when the stakes are exponentially high and there is serious risk for extensive liability do we think about using mediators. If people use mediators on smaller, more personal issues, the initial instinct is to conclude that they must not be terribly mature because they are letting others fight their battles for them. To unpack this innate prejudice, I think it is helpful to look at God the Father. Far from being a weakling, he is all powerful and omniscient. When we as his children went astray and when he was angry and in conflict with us, how did he choose to resolve the situation?

The stunning answer to that question is Jesus Christ! First Timothy 2:5 says, "For there is one God, and one mediator also between God and men, the man Christ Jesus." Hebrews 7–8 outlines how this mediation occurred and how Christ initiated a new covenant between humankind and God. God also chose to use priests throughout the Old Testament to mediate between God and humans. And when God wanted to bring the children of Israel out of Egypt, he chose Moses to be the mediator.[6] If God himself uses mediation, should we not respect this method too?

Third-party mediators can be profoundly helpful when there is tension about money in a ministry or cross-cultural partnership. Because disagreements about money can trigger such strong emotion, third party mediators can help everyone stay calm and can prevent cross-cultural partners from saying or doing things they will later regret. It is important to know, however, that there is no "one right way" to do mediation. In fact, one doctoral student sought to uncover the common practices of mediation solely in one section of Gambia. At the conclusion of all his research, he realized there was no one preset or prescribed way to do it even within that one specific context.[7] The same mediators would often tailor their process and work differently with different people. The key is having someone who is trusted by both sides and who will maintain confidentiality.

My colleagues working in Latin America developed a department called Reconciliation and Unity.[8] They chose this name as they felt it evoked a more positive image than a department called Conflict Management. In essence what they found was that for the Scriptures to truly reach all people in Latin America, there had to be unprecedented cooperation between diverse groups and denominations. Since many of these people had never worked together, they knew there would be conflict and there needed to be a way to work through it in a healthy way that facilitated stronger partnerships. By creating a department to address this need, it took some of the shame out of the situation when disagreements arose. There is a person heading up the department with extensive linguistic and peace-making skills who can act as the go-between to help partners resolve differences while progressing toward their goals.

ONE-DOWN POSITION

When conflict arises over money, it is common for partners to instinctively begin to play the "power" card. However, instead of trying to dominate another partner or use threats to obtain or coerce a desired outcome, the one-down position is often much more effective. In this method the partner communicates vulnerability and asks the other person to help them so they are not shamed and do not lose face. In one parable Jesus tells us about a slave who mishandled funds. The approach used by the slave is a somewhat dramatic version of the one-down position. It is illustrated in Matthew 18:26-27. The action taken by the slave resolved the conflict, until later when the business owner realized he was not sincere. That is the critical thing to remember with this method, as with the others as well. If we utilize any conflict resolution method as a way to simply manipulate others, over time our disingenuousness will be uncovered. And when that happens, it will only make a bad situation worse.

The one-down position can be quite beneficial for people in cross-cultural partnerships. It is an especially helpful way to resolve a problem when the person who reports to donors is being hurt by untimely reports or by funds being misallocated to different purposes. It will be most effective if you use terminology that your cross-cultural partner can understand.

A number of years ago, I was getting more and more angry that reports were not being prepared promptly despite my constant requests. Finally, I sat down with the person responsible for generating these. I explained how vulnerable I was, and how much I would lose face if I could not provide to top leaders what was being asked of me. I explained that they took a risk when they put me in this role. I explained that I was younger than other leaders, and they might regret their decision and I might lose my job. It was utterly amazing. From that point on reports were delivered timely or early. If there was any hint of a delay, I was told about it well before the target date. I was then able to tell the people to whom I reported the reason why a specific deadline could not be met, and the reasons were always wholly logical and legitimate.

Why did I choose this method to resolve the conflict? I needed this person to protect my face. I would incur incredible shame if things continued as they were progressing. As a higher status person in the culture, I needed that person's help and cooperation or there would be very negative consequences for me. I could have responded with anger, accusing and maligning the person or issuing threats. I was in a position of power. However, I was astounded at the incredibly better outcome it produced, both for fiscal accountability and for my ministry relationships. The only caveat is that if this method is used inappropriately or too often, it can open the door for others to take advantage of you. Discernment is needed to determine the best conflict-resolution method to utilize in any given situation.

STORY TELLING

I am amazed at how effective Africans are at using stories to get across some of the most complex and profound truths. I have heard of stories being used many times by Majority World leaders to communicate the dangers of theft and the fact that it will not be tolerated. At times a single well-placed story can solve an incredibly complex problem.

I have seen this backfire, however, when Majority World leaders use this style with Western pastors or missionaries who are not at all versed in this skill. I am not sure how else to say it except by being direct. Sometimes Westerners do not get the real meaning behind the story. I cannot count the number of times I have had discussions with friends who said, "I sensed in my soul that there was a deeper meaning they were conveying, but I have no idea what it was!"

Does Scripture give us any insight into this dilemma? The story of Nathan confronting David about his sin with Bathsheba is full of helpful lessons. Nathan told David a compelling story about the unjust act of an exceedingly wealthy person against a noble yet poor man. David was incensed by the story and told Nathan, "As the LORD lives, surely the man who has done this deserves to die" (2 Samuel 12:5). I often wonder what Nathan was thinking. Was he wondering, *What in the heck is wrong with this guy? How can he be so dense and not see that I am talking about him?* But Nathan persisted. When he realized that David was not "getting it" he switched gears. At that moment he began speaking directly to David, helping him to see his sin.

As Majority World leaders work with leaders from other Western countries, it is good to use stories to confront issues that need to be dealt with and resolved. However, Scripture gives us an example here that encourages us to take it one step further. As we discussed earlier, we cannot assume that the other person will make the right meaning of an incident or story. If there is a chance that they do not get it, we need to move past our comfort zone and speak directly like Nathan illustrates in this text.

PUBLIC SHAMING

Although it can be direct or indirect, public shaming is incredibly powerful in some situations. Jesus uses this method with the Pharisees in Matthew 23. In direct verbal confrontations he calls them hypocrites, fools and blind guides. He seems to have taken these extreme measures because of the extreme hardness of their hearts. Sometimes profound stubbornness and rationalization can only be broken with such measures. Christ's words of public shaming were intended as a rebuke. However, I think in his soul he truly wished they would finally "get it."

Paul also used public shaming, although in a more indirect manner. He never mentions the names of the people involved, but in his first letter to the Corinthian church he writes, "It is actually reported that there is immorality among you, and immorality of such a kind as does not exist even among the Gentiles, that someone has his father's wife" (1 Corinthians 5:1). He continues to ask the community to not associate with this person so the man will bear the repercussions of his wrongful behavior. By the second letter to the Corinthians we see this public shaming was effective in changing the abhorrent behavior. Paul writes, "Sufficient for such a one is this punishment which was inflicted by the majority, so that on the contrary you should rather forgive and comfort him, otherwise such a one might be overwhelmed by excessive sorrow. Wherefore I urge you to reaffirm your love for him" (2 Corinthians 2:6-8).

Sometimes Majority World leaders find public shaming to be quite effective in curtailing embezzlement. David Augsburger, author of the book *Conflict Mediation Across Cultures*, talks about two fascinating ways that public shaming is used in Africa. In one community when theft takes place, everyone in the community just talks about the sin all the time. They never say the name of the person they expect committed the act, but over and over they talk about what a horrible act it was and how it damaged the community. The person feels so overwhelmed by the shame he no longer commits the act![9] He also mentions the Mbuti tribe in East Africa. They use mime to act out the sin and transgression of a person who stole cattle from a weaker man in the village. Through drama and humor they take the tension out of the situation while publicly shaming and scorning the inappropriate behavior that damages community.[10]

COVERING ANOTHER

Covering a person is an interesting option when conflict arises. At times it is the appropriate solution. If a person normally does a good job but they drop the ball occasionally, it is often appropriate for another person to "take the heat" to facilitate a better long-term outcome. An example is when a reporting deadline is missed. A Western partner can simply choose to apologize and leave it at that, instead of sharing all the details that their non-Western partner did not complete the paperwork on time. Jesus covers our sin with his blood so we all experience this act of grace daily.

SILENCE

Silence can speak volumes. The act of silence can be an incredibly powerful and intense response in conflict. Jesus exercised this approach when he was brought before his accusers. He said very little or nothing at all. In Matthew 26:57-64 and Matthew 27:11-12 we see that silence enraged his accusers. We are not sure exactly why Jesus chose this option. Perhaps he felt it was a waste of time to express himself? They had made their decision anyway? The outcome was not going to change? Another possibility is that it was a way for Jesus to exert incredible power while being in what seemed to be a powerless situation.

Silence is an option available to us, but it needs to be used with care since the message to the other person can easily become distorted. I have seen indigenous leaders use silence when they are being asked questions about financial accountability. Although they might have every right to be angry about any number of issues, choosing silence almost always makes the situation worse. In this situation we see it at the end of Christ's life. He was not concerned about salvaging these relationships. When money is involved, I do not usually see a good outcome when partners are unwilling to answer important questions. Often what is interpreted on the other side is extremely negative and frequently worse than the true situation. As a conflict management method, I have seen it cause cross-cultural partnerships to deteriorate quite quickly.

CONTEXTUALIZE YOUR CONFLICT MANAGEMENT PROCESSES

Stella Ting-Toomey writes, "Conflict exists as part of the human condition. It is an inescapable phenomenon in all societal organizations."[11] Despite the obvious validity of such a statement, many partners are caught off-guard when conflict occurs. They unknowingly enter ministry partnerships with the false assumption things will go smoothly and collaboration will be easy. An article written by Jeff Weiss and Jonathan Hughes, published in the *Harvard Business Review,* is a more accurate description of the situation. They write, "That fact is, you can't improve collaboration until you've addressed the issue of conflict. This can come as a surprise to even the most experienced executives. . . . And even if they do recognize this, many mistakenly assume that efforts to increase collaboration will significantly reduce conflict, when in fact some of these efforts . . . actually produce more of it."[12]

Working more closely in collaboration raises dissimilarities to an even greater pitch. Things can be more easily tolerated when we do not spend a lot of time together and when we do not have to actively engage together to get a task done. Amidst the stress of meeting deadlines and benchmarks, what would normally be insignificant differences can begin to feel like insurmountable obstacles.

John Paul Lederach is a renowned voice in the cross-cultural reconciliation movement. He writes, "The complexity of authentic reconciliation emerges from the capacity of people to build on an appropriate process, created and owned by them, rather than the rote application of preconceived processes."[13] I cannot give you a "one size fits all" package about the best way to resolve conflict in all cross-cultural partnerships. However, I do believe if you take the time to dialogue and examine the topic together with your cross-cultural partners, you will be able to design methods that will work wonderfully for many years to come.

A JAPANESE AND JAVANESE WAY

David Augsburger writes:

> There are cultures, the Japanese and the Javanese, to name two obvious examples, that do not value dialectic argumentative patterns. Where harmony and cooperation are basic values, verbal contradiction is not the automatic first choice in conflict. A more accepted process is to affirm the strengths of each other's position, let them stand without attack, and then join in exploring other options. Both parties search for superior options. . . . If a superior alternative is not found, the previous positions remain undestroyed. Frequently the old positions are essentially good—they cannot be simply discredited, but they are no longer necessary.[14]

Often when conflict arises we hold to a paradigm that one person is right and the other is wrong. In cross-cultural partnership, that paradigm is not helpful. Both processes might be "right" given distinctive contexts. However, neither approach might work for collaborative efforts across cultures. The goal is not to demean or disrespect approaches that have worked for hundreds of years. Instead, the challenge is to find new ways of working through conflict that will foster healthy and strong relationships now and into the future.

MISSED OPPORTUNITIES

If we rely solely upon "words" to resolve conflicts, we miss out on a great number of wonderful opportunities to illustrate the gospel of Christ in the world. One instance that comes to mind is a story told by a leader from Cameroon.[15] He said to be healed or reconciled with an enemy in his culture you follow a very specific practice. A mediator grinds bitter herbs into a very fine powder. Then each party tastes of the ground powder and that means the enmity is ended. For me that story is powerful and reminiscent of the message of Communion, Christ's body being broken for us to eat in remembrance of him.

Augsburger tells a different story about a people group from India. There the way you know if reconciliation has taken place is that every person takes a drink from a jug of palm beer. If there are no drinks, that means reconciliation has not taken place.[16] This too reminds me of the Communion table when Jesus spoke of sharing his blood. We are also to drink in remembrance of him to symbolize our forgiveness and reconciliation with God the Father and with one another.

We shortchange ourselves and others by not taking time to truly learn how reconciliation is handled most effectively in different contexts. If we look at the whole of Scripture, we see there are multiple options and combinations of methods that may be employed. It is good to keep this in mind as we move on to the next topic regarding misallocated funding.

OPTIONS IF DESIGNATED FUNDS ARE MISALLOCATED

I am not aware of many situations more ripe for destructive conflict than when donor-designated funding is spent for different purposes. Here, more than in almost any other situation, how we go about making meaning becomes critical. It is very easy to jump to extremely negative conclusions about another person when such judgments might be totally incorrect. When we look at attribution theory, the research indicates that those working at a distance from one another are more prone to making negative and faulty attributions and assumptions about each other's motives or intentions. Excessive care needs to be taken to avoid prematurely jumping to erroneous conclusions.

STAY CALM

When funds appear to be misallocated or inappropriately diverted to an unauthorized expense or program, it is easy to lose your cool. I have seen people who are normally quite patient and easygoing get incredibly volatile in this situation. It is important to first consider if, when you initially established the partnership, you agreed on how you would resolve future conflict. If you have outlined a process, honor it in this situation. Do not begin talking poorly about anyone. Do not begin voicing disapproval or disgust at the partner's behavior.

Instead, go initially through the mediator or follow the steps outlined in your original conflict management process. If your partner sees you following these agreed upon procedures even though you are upset, it will build trust in your relationship and heighten the likelihood for a positive outcome. Remember the big picture. You are working to help build the kingdom of God. God's purposes will not be advanced if you lose your temper and bring shame upon yourself and others. Sometimes God uses trials to help fashion our character. We need to remember that we live in a fallen world, and difficulties are a normal aspect of our work and ministry lives. If we stay calm and practice some healthy self-talk,[1] we will be much more clearheaded and able to discern God's wisdom for the situation.

SUSPEND JUDGMENT, ASK QUESTIONS AND LISTEN

If you did not establish a protocol for resolving conflict when you started the partnership, it is critical that you do everything within your power to ensure a good outcome. While staying calm, it is important to suspend judgment. You cannot judge the situation because you do not have all the facts. Even if there have been problems in the past, the reasons for this situation could be entirely different. You need to exercise wisdom, begin asking questions and listen carefully. These are the types of questions you need answers to before you can know how to proceed.

- Was there a lack of true understanding? Is the concept of donor-designated funding new in this context or new for this group of leaders?

- Was it simply an honest mistake without any malice or ill intent?

- If it was an honest mistake, does the partner seem willing and able to correct it? If they do not have funds to correct it, do you sense they would correct it if they could?

- Where did the funds go? Did it truly help someone with an emergency? What outcome was achieved by using the funding in this way?

- What was "gained" by the person who misappropriated funds? What ramifications would he or she have faced if the action had not been taken?

- How is misappropriation of designated funds viewed within the Christian community in that context? Is designated funding a new concept or a familiar and honored one?

- How do community or church leaders deal with this type of situation if funds are misallocated?

- Was "selfish gain" part of the equation? Was the act motivated by greed or by love?

The goal behind these questions is to try to get at the heart of why this happened. It is necessary to discern, as best you can, why this was done. You cannot make an assessment of the situation or know how to proceed without this information.

THE DIFFERENCE BETWEEN THE FRUIT AND THE BREAD

Earlier we discussed the story of Adam and Eve and how they dishonored God by using fruit from the tree of the knowledge of good and evil for their own purpose. There were enormous ramifications. Their relationship with God was altered, their freedom was curtailed, and the level of blessings they experienced from the relationship was significantly reduced. However, in Matthew 12:1-7 we see another instance of food being misallocated for a different purpose, and there were no serious repercussions. Instead, God seemed to provide an allowance in this situation:

> At that time Jesus went through the grainfields on the Sabbath, and His disciples became hungry and began to pick the heads of grain and eat. But when the Pharisees saw this, they said to Him, "Look, Your disciples do what is not lawful to do on a Sabbath." But he said to them, "Have you not read what David did when he became hungry, he and his companions, how he entered the house of God, and they ate the consecrated bread, which was not lawful for him to eat nor for those with him, but for the priests alone? Or have you not read in the Law, that on the Sabbath the priests in the temple break the Sabbath and are innocent? But I say to you that something greater than the temple is here. But if you had known what this means, 'I desire compassion, and not a sacrifice,' you would not have condemned the innocent."

God judged Adam and Eve for eating the fruit that was designated for a different purpose, but he did not judge David. Why? It is clear from this passage and the corresponding text in 1 Samuel 21:1-10 that there were extenuating circumstances. The reason David disobeyed a commandment he would normally honor was because King Saul, whom God appointed, was persecuting David unjustly. For this reason, David had to flee for his life through no fault of his own. He was now a hungry refugee, who needed sustenance to be able to outrun Saul and his men. God had plans for David, great plans. He had anointed him and was using him greatly. David had a future that was important to God's overall mission in the world. In a similar way, so too did the disciples. They were eating the grain permitted to be gleaned, but they were doing it at what would normally be considered the wrong time. However, they were hungry and they needed sustenance to continue.

THE REASON BEHIND THE ACTION SHOULD BE WHAT INFORMS OUR RESPONSE

What are we trying to figure out? The motive behind the action is what God cares about and so, for that reason, we need to care about it as well. Was the partner's misstep caused by a lack of understanding of designated funding because it was such a new concept? If so, there will be a bit of a learning curve that has to take place. However, with thoughtful and caring dialogue you can work through this hurdle. Were the funds used for ministry? If so, perhaps the overarching outcome actually accomplished the same purpose for which the donor gave the funds. Sometimes what appears to be a misallocation of funding turns out to be perfectly legitimate behavior. In these instances, it is the funding partner that needs to be trained and educated so they do not become unnecessarily upset.

How does the community perceive the situation? Do they understand what happened and why it is so serious? If not, is there a way you can talk with them and their leaders so they can understand the situation you are in when this happens? If there is a way that they can keep you from experiencing shame, they might be willing to take extra steps and precautions even if it is different from how they normally handle things. In this case, the original "problem" can open up opportunities for deeper dialogue that will build even greater trust with one another.

Also, what situation was the person in who misallocated funding? Would the fallout have been so damaging if he had not taken the action that his own ministry and credibility would have been on the line? If so, is there a broader need that the partnership should be addressing? And if this need cannot be met under the restrictions of your nonprofit status, can another partner be brought into the relationship whose nonprofit status with the IRS or other governmental body enables them to do that kind of ministry or provide that kind of service? By working creatively to find a long-term solution to the original issue, it is possible to lessen the likelihood of this type of thing occurring again. Only if it was done from a heart of blatant greed, or if there is blatant disregard to how this will negatively affect your own organization should there be a warning issued or a threat to end the partnership.

FAITHFULNESS IN THE LITTLE THINGS

Faithfulness is such an important quality and so necessary for cross-cultural ministry partnerships to flourish and do great things for God. As the funding partner, are you being faithful? Are you delivering on your promises? Are you doing what you said you would do? As the Majority World partner overseeing the ministry and working in your context, are you being faithful? Are you using financial resources as you promised? Are you doing your part to help make sure your cross-cultural partner is not going to suffer harmful legal action because of your behavior?

I think Matthew 25:21 can be a great guide as we enter into cross-cultural ministry partnerships. Jesus says in this parable that if we are faithful with the little things, he will put us in charge of many things. He first checks to see if we are faithful with smaller amounts of responsibility and resources, and then he progresses from there. The ministries I have seen get into the deepest trouble in cross-cultural partnerships are those that from the outset choose to partner on a grand scale. They might agree on a quarter-of-a-million-dollar project for the first initiative, never really knowing each other or working in tandem together. Then, when things go badly, there is much at stake. Sometimes the fiscal credibility of both organizations becomes damaged beyond repair.

Why choose to start with grandiose schemes? Jesus tells us we should first be faithful with little things and then he will give us more. Why, then do we not hold ourselves to that same standard? It is a logical one. We are all growing and maturing along the way. We are all learning from our mistakes, hopefully, and becoming better mission practitioners and leaders. Why not follow his way in this area and save ourselves unnecessary stress and ulcers! When we start small and learn from our mistakes, our organizations are not put in jeopardy. The way we "do" ministry needs to be informed by Scripture. This is one application that has tremendous applicability for cross-cultural ministry partnerships.

WE NEED WISDOM

These are core issues to consider when funds are misallocated for purposes other than those designated by the donor. However, there is another scenario that sometimes happens in ministry that is also difficult. It is managing the fallout after fraud and embezzlement are uncovered. We will examine this issue next.

Options If Embezzlement
or Fraud Occurs

When embezzlement or fraud occurs, it is easy to feel overwhelmed. A leader of a global church-planting mission once told me that after all his years of service, the issue that was most draining and upsetting was when he found out his accountant was stealing from the ministry. In that instance, it was an American missionary committing the fraud overseas.

It is easy when fraud and embezzlement are uncovered to feel betrayed. It is also common in those moments, if you are a leader, to feel sorry for yourself. Often you are already making a lot of sacrifices to work in missions; you are overworked and underpaid. You are juggling so many different roles it is hard to keep your sanity in the best of times—now this too! It is easy to go down a path of self-pity, but in the long run it will not help. Instead, it is important to not let your emotions get the best of you. You need to keep a clear head so you can effectively lead your colleagues and organization through this experience in a way that honors God and lessens any additional damage to his kingdom.

EVEN JESUS HAD TO DEAL WITH EMBEZZLEMENT

Perhaps it helps if we remember that even our Lord had to deal with the situation of one of his closest friends and colleagues embezzling ministry funds. Scripture describes this in John 12:1-6. As the story unfolds, Mary pours a pound of costly perfume to anoint the feet of Jesus. Judas seemed offended that this lavish perfume was not sold for the equivalent of eleven months' wages and given to the poor. The critique might seem logical to many of us who at times feel believers are not terribly good stewards of the funds and resources entrusted to them. However, was the motivation for this comment pure? Verse 6 says, "Now he said this, not because he was concerned about the poor, but because he was a thief, and as he had the money box, he used to pilfer what was put into it."

As if Jesus did not have enough on his plate to manage, he also had one of his closest friends stealing money from his ministry. Sadly, dealing with the reality of fraud or embezzlement is not terribly rare. Be careful with the amount of self-pity and heartache you choose to bear. Most of the time when people choose to sin all we can do is manage the fallout.

AN OUNCE OF PREVENTION

As a leader, whether from the West or the Majority World, you are responsible for creating a safe work environment for your colleagues. It is therefore incumbent upon you to take the steps necessary to create the healthiest work place possible. God cares about how we utilize resources but he cares deeply about people as well. If fraud occurs it will have ripple effects that will affect not only the person who stole funds but his or her family, their community, other colleagues, and even wider circles of people. Howard Silverstone and Howard Davia have been experts in fraud prevention for many years. They wrote the book *Fraud 101*.[1] In it they explain that leaders need to have

> an effective prevention and detection strategy. The elements of such a strategy include the need to
>
> - Understand why fraud is committed.
> - Ensure that factors that may motivate employees to commit fraud are minimized.
> - Understand the opportunities for fraud in the business.
> - Pinpoint the exposures and high-risk areas and reduce the opportunities for fraud.
> - Know the symptoms of fraud.
> - Communicate expected behavior to employees.
> - Respond appropriately to indentified problems and seek appropriate sanctions against the perpetrators.[2]

Since the method of how fraud can occur is so incredibly diverse, it is best to develop a process that is contextualized for the culture and people involved. I do not think it is effective to go into a new context and lecture about the importance of fiscal integrity. Instead, it is more helpful if a trusted person can facilitate a dialogue that enables the group to come to shared conclusions about fiscal integrity. Often simply walking people through a series of questions can help them begin to describe what has happened in their culture and what steps need to be taken to protect the ministry from fraud. To help with this process, appendix B has been designed as a starting place for such a discussion.

We will never know most people's areas of deepest struggle and personal temptation. We only know that, as humans, every person has them.

The tone you set as a leader will permeate your entire ministry.

If this is not a priority to you, if it is not discussed and financial controls are lax, there is a much higher probability that embezzlement will occur. If that is the case, you are partially responsible for letting it happen. Perhaps it would be helpful to share three stories so you can begin to think through this issue.

THE MINISTRY'S RESTAURANT

When I was working overseas, a ministry contacted me for help. Michael, the new director, had a bad feeling that his accountant might be stealing from the organization. He had no proof, just a bad feeling. He asked if I would be willing to come and attend a meeting with their accountant and some of their administrators. They were in the process of doing a software conversion, and it was proving to be a good avenue for looking more carefully at each account and its corresponding history.

I arrived and was introduced to the team. For much of the time I listened as different issues were raised. When asked about specific accounts, I expressed that they seemed appropriate. In the first part of the day as things played out I was not sure if Michael had cause for alarm. However, later in the day I was taken to the ministry's restaurant where I was served a nice lunch. I saw many people coming and going, and I was told the restaurant served approximately three hundred people each day. By all accounts, it was sizeable operation. Volunteers often manned the enterprise, or young people were paid a minimum wage to staff it.

After lunch we went back into the meeting, and I began scanning the chart of accounts. Nowhere on that chart were there accounts for the ministry's restaurant. I asked Joel, the accountant, where these accounts were located. It was then that Joel started to move around in his seat and for the first time he would not look at me when he spoke. He said the restaurant was "off the books." I asked, "Why is the restaurant off the books? Isn't it important to have all the ministry's programs and projects on the books so there are good financial controls and policies in place, and so managers can track expenses, understand trends and so forth?" I explained that if something is off the books it cannot be managed effectively. If expenses are tracked, managers can see if they begin to spike and can determine the cause. If they get reports they might begin to discuss other ways the restaurant can be used to generate even more income. But nowhere in any of the financial reports was there even an income or an expense line for the restaurant.

Joel said, "The restaurant does not make any money. It always breaks even so there is no reason to include it with the other reports." The afternoon progressed. There were a couple of other small issues that arose, but nothing as material as the restaurant. As a CPA, I felt the restaurant was the area most vulnerable to theft as it was a cash-based enterprise and there were no formal cash registers or software to track income or inventory. Afterward I gave Michael my take on the situation. I said he needed to begin investigating in detail the restaurant as I felt it a likely scenario that fraud was occurring in that area. Joel, being a trained accountant, knew that I understood that the restaurant would be the most vulnerable area. However, whenever the topic was raised, he seemed to be extremely evasive.

A friend who had also attended the meeting later said, "Oh, Mary, you are so suspicious. I don't know what they taught you when you became a CPA. I think you need to let your heart rule. Joel is a wonderful guy. He is just distracted because he is being sent by his church soon to be a missionary in a remote country. God is really raising him up to be a leading missionary from his local church here. Your suspicion is totally unwarranted." I told her that I hoped I was wrong for everyone's sake but that I did not think that I was.

Two weeks later Joel quit the mission, left his wife and moved in with his girlfriend, whom he had been supporting on the side for more than two years. I believe he funded the additional household from resources he skimmed from the restaurant. However, since there were no records kept, the scope of the fraud could not be wholly determined. In the months that followed the restaurant always made a substantial profit.

The ministry felt they had enough information to take legal action against him. Since they deeply loved his wife, they felt some disciplinary measures needed to be taken. The last time I spoke with the administrator leading the organization, this was how they were going to pursue the situation.

THE MOST GODLY WOMAN I EVER MET

The second scenario is quite different. I had a friend who was the CFO for a large ministry. I used to travel extensively with my job, and whenever I traveled to that country and arrived in the capital, I would always call her to see if she would like to get together for dinner. Often I would go to her office before it closed, we would chat for a while about any number of things, and then we would leave. This friend was always working a lot of hours, and she was happy to know another missionary accountant whom she could talk to about complex finance issues.

Each time I called or visited her office, I was greeted by a woman who seemed like the most godly person I had ever met. She was so kind, gracious and loving. It was as though—and this is no exaggeration at all—she exuded God. There was this aura about her that radiated the Holy Spirit. The thing that I felt was even more uncanny was that whenever I called, even if there had been a three- or four-month lag in communication, as soon as I said "Hi, is . . ." she would say, "Hi, Mary! How are you? I will get Becky for you!"

This—without the aid of caller ID! With two words uttered she always knew when it was me on the other end. I thought, *Wow—I wish I could be more like her! I wish I could love God so much that it literally exuded from me like that!* I actually used to pray that God would help me to be more like this woman. She seemed utterly extraordinary to me.

A few years later, I found out from my friend that she uncovered a scam that this woman had been carrying out for years. She was handling all the shipping for the ministry. She found a way to alter the receipts and documentation to show a higher price than what she actually paid at the post office. The amount of extra money she was raising was fairly significant based on a typical salary in that country. My friend said she wanted to fire her on the spot, but another leader in her organization wanted to give her a warning and another chance. The woman wept in a heartfelt way, seemed truly contrite, and promised to never do it again. My friend caught her a second time doing the same thing, and she said she buttoned everything down so tight there was no possible way the woman could ever get away with anything again. A few weeks later the receptionist quit. She said she had to find a job where she could earn more money! I am not a gambling person, but if I were, my. odds would be that she embezzles again.

THE MISSION BOOKKEEPER

I have a close friend, Steve, whom I have known for many years. No one ever thought Steve would become a missionary. But much to everyone's surprise, God called him to reach out and develop leaders in northern Africa. He was training young pastors who, after graduation, were serving in many different nations. When my friend started working in missions, it was an enormous pay cut. Prior to this he had been a successful businessperson. Living on support was meager at times, and he felt the financial pinch regularly, especially as his family grew.

While Steve was visiting and we were catching up on old times he said, "Mary, I have a story for you!" He told me that Jill, the person doing the bookkeeping for the small agency that sent him overseas, was caught stealing from his support. A small church in the Midwest established his mission agency. Despite its small size, it was influencing many nations and doing great work. The church hired Jill to do the bookkeeping as a way to help build her morale and provide a salary to help meet her needs. Jill had been married to a pastor whose name was Paul. Paul had committed adultery, disobeyed God, left Jill, resigned from ministry and was now married to his former mistress, Susie. In the midst of Jill's heartache over the unfairness of what had transpired in her life, her only daughter, Alison, was getting married. Alison was marrying Walt and Eleanor's son Zak. Walt and Eleanor were the pastoral couple who started the church mission agency through which my friend Steve did his work in Africa.

As Alison's wedding date drew closer, Jill was overcome with grief that she could not provide enough financial resources to help her daughter have a nicer wedding and reception. Jill began telling herself a lie over time that is quite common when people embezzle funds. She told herself that she would just "borrow" money from the ministry. In time she would pay it back and everything would be OK. This would enable her to help Alison so she too did not have to incur the shame and embarrassment brought about by her father's infidelity and unfaithfulness. Alison was marrying into such a good family. Jill did not want her daughter to have to bear the negative repercussions of her father's sin.

Jill began stealing funds from the ministry and channeling them unknowingly to Alison to help with wedding expenses. However, over time she was caught. Walt and Eleanor were shaken to the core. "How could this happen? What will this mean for our son marrying Alison? What will this mean to our family relationships and to our church members who have given sacrificially for so long to this important outreach?" Everywhere they looked there were negative repercussions. They did not know how to proceed, but they prayed for wisdom.

In the end they reported the crime to the police. The legal authorities and the mission's board of directors granted Jill the option of repaying her debt over time rather than going to prison. They fired Jill as the bookkeeper, and they implemented tighter financial controls so the likelihood of any fraud in the future would be greatly reduced. However, Walt and Eleanor then extended an extraordinary offer. They told Jill that she could live with them rent free as she paid back the debt.

Jill accepted their gracious offer. When Jill made her last payment to cover what had been taken, the church threw a huge party to celebrate how God had redeemed the incident. Relationships were deepened, and Jill could go forward with a clean conscience, knowing she had made full restitution and was fully forgiven. After paying off the debt, Jill continued living with Walt and Eleanor for another year before striking out on her own. Their family is closer than ever. My friend Steve said these words:

> You know, when I first found out she was stealing from us I was really mad. Here I was struggling like crazy to pay bills and meet the needs of my family. It was already hard and she was making it even more difficult. But I've got to give it to Walt and Eleanor. The way they handled it was extraordinary. They wanted to model godly reconciliation since the believers in our part of the world were overcoming such difficult circumstances to learn to live in peace with people

who were once their enemies. I think in the end it has been a good experience for the mission, for the church and for everyone involved.

RED FLAGS

In many situations there are red flags that should trigger in us questions about fraud. Sometimes in other countries people make subtle hints or drop subtle clues that something bad is happening. The sad thing, though, is that as Westerners we often do not pick up on the cues. Afterward Majority World colleagues think, *We tried to warn them. I guess they have so much money they just don't care.* When this happens, a culture of fraud will begin to permeate the entire organization.

Changes in income levels, lots of new purchases, changes in lifestyle—all of these are indicators of which we need to watch and be aware. Unwillingness to let someone examine work, an unwillingness to ever go on vacation, and unwillingness to let someone else do the purchasing or receipting—these too are important clues. When cross-cultural ministry is taking place, it is wise to have a mediator that indigenous colleagues feel they can safely approach. Often they will not want to approach a Western leader, for to tell him or her that someone is stealing would cause a loss of face. Having no avenue available simply fosters a culture of silence, and problems that need to be addressed will continue much longer than necessary.

THERE IS NO "ONE RIGHT WAY" TO DEAL WITH EMBEZZLEMENT

The third story is by far the most inspirational. Many will think that Walt and Eleanor took these steps just because Jill was now going to be a part of their family through marriage. However, the motivation for their sacrificial offer was steeped in a desire to model godly reconciliation. They were profoundly affected by the grace their cross-cultural partners were showing toward past enemies. Walt and Eleanor wanted to model this in America as well. We should not relegate extensive and creative solutions that require personal sacrifice merely to those with whom we are related by physical blood lines or marriage. We are all family. We are all brothers and sisters in the kingdom of God.

However, there is no one-size-fits-all approach to dealing with theft or fraud when it occurs. People's hearts differ, true contrition over sin differs, and circumstances behind actions differ. Some ministries have a "no tolerance under any circumstance" rule, and they clearly explain that they will legally prosecute any person caught embezzling or committing fraud. Some opt to move the colleague to a different role where he or she has no access to funds of any kind. They choose this course because the person is so gifted and valuable, to lose him or her would be to great a setback for the ministry as a whole. Some choose to just fire the person and not give a reference if future employers call and ask. Others seek to resolve it through a network of extended relatives and allow public shame to take its course. Others seek elders in the indigenous church, and they opt to follow their advice as to whether or not to press criminal charges.

TAKING PROACTIVE STEPS

I believe in proactive measures. I think it is good to talk through what will happen if embezzlement or fraud occurs long before it actually does occur. It is wise to get those involved in the ministry to help brainstorm the ways fraud might be carried out in that context and the reasons why colleagues might stumble. Together we can then create and design controls that are needed for each unique context. (See appendix B.) By addressing the issue in this way, there is organizational ownership by everyone, and it becomes a natural outgrowth of the organizational culture. Everyone knows that the measures are being taken so people will not stumble, relationships will not be disrupted, ministry programs will not be hindered, and the name of Christ will be held in high esteem by unbelievers observing the ministry.

KEEPING OUR EYES FOCUSED ON SCRIPTURE

Managing conflict is not fun. However, we can learn from our mistakes and get better at navigating it in redemptive ways. Lest we lose heart and think that ministry is supposed to be easy, it might be good to examine Philippians 2:1-16. In this passage we will find both the encouragement and exhortation we need to be better partners!

HOW TO TELL IF CHRIST
IS LORD OF YOUR PARTNERSHIP

When I was a young believer, I was often challenged to reflect on whether Christ was both my Savior and my Lord. All human beings appreciate the Savior part. We like grace and being forgiven. We like gifts and blessings and joy. But what about that Lord part? That is where it gets hard. That is where there is a call to sacrifice and to suffer and at times even to die. My first inclination is that the lordship of Christ does not sound fun or appealing. However, there is a profound spiritual reality I have seen time and time again over the years: only when we walk in the lordship of Jesus can we exude a lasting brightness in a world full of darkness. It is when Christ is both our Savior and our Lord that the power of God is seen amidst our weaknesses. It is at this place where God often chooses to do spectacular things through his children.

If we take this concept of lordship as our vision for partnership, what might it look like? How might we know if Christ is truly

Lord of our missions work and cross-cultural partnerships? I think Philippians 2:1-16 gives us a clear and compelling picture that we can use as a plumb line to determine if this is the case. Here is what the apostle Paul exhorts:

Therefore if there is any encouragement in Christ, if there is any consolation of love, if there is any fellowship of the Spirit, if any affection and compassion, make my joy complete by being of the same mind, maintaining the same love, united in spirit, intent on one purpose. Do nothing from selfishness or empty conceit, but with humility of mind regard one another as more important than yourselves; do not merely look out for your own personal interests, but also for the interests of others. Have this attitude in yourselves which was also in Christ Jesus, who, although He existed in the form of God, did not regard equality with God a thing to be grasped, but emptied Himself, taking the form of a bond-servant, and being made in the likeness of men. Being found in appearance as a man, He humbled Himself by becoming obedient to the point of death, even death on a cross. For this reason also, God highly exalted Him, and bestowed on Him, the name which is above every name, so that at the name of Jesus EVERY KNEE WILL BOW, of those who are in heaven and on earth and under the earth, and that every tongue confess that Jesus Christ is Lord, to the glory of God the Father. So then, my beloved, just as you have always obeyed, not as in my presence only, but now much more in my absence, work out your salvation with fear and trembling; for it is God who is at work in you, both to will and to work for His good pleasure. Do all things without grumbling or disputing; so that you will prove yourselves to be blameless and innocent, children of God above reproach in the midst of a crooked and

perverse generation, among whom you appear as lights in
the world, holding fast the word of life, so that in the day of
Christ I will have reason to glory because I did not run in
vain nor toil in vain.

How does such a passage apply to cross-cultural ministry partnerships? How might it look if we applied the principles from this
passage to the way we work with one another? Here are key principles I see from this text.

1. *Intensely and actively look for the good in each other.* Verse 1:
"Therefore if there is *any* encouragement in Christ, if there is *any*
consolation of love, if there is *any* fellowship of the Spirit, if *any*
affection and compassion."

It is so easy to obsess on what we do not have in common and
what we dislike about how another person works. Paul starts
this passage by exhorting us to intentionally focus and look for
any signs of encouragement, *any* love, *any* fellowship, *any* affection and *any* compassion in one another. By focusing on these
things, we will bring out the best in one another instead of the
worst. *Are you intensely and actively looking for the good in your
cross-cultural partner?*

2. *Stay focused on the bigger issues you have in common.* Verse
2: "make my joy complete by being of the same mind, maintaining
the same love, united in spirit, intent on one purpose."

I am often amazed as I sit with my Wycliffe colleagues and
partners around the world. Churches split so often over minute
differences in doctrine, and yet my organization experiences unity
amidst such diverse peoples with such diverse beliefs and convictions. How do we experience this depth of unity? Perhaps it is
because we are all working toward the goal of helping to get Scripture into the hands of people around the world in their own heart
languages. For that reason, when it comes to Christian doctrine

we choose to focus on what we have in common. We covenant on the front end to intentionally focus on the big picture, those core doctrinal truths that are true for all believers. Since we stay on that level, the less significant doctrinal issues do not become material for contentious arguments. They simply are not an issue. If we focus on the bigger picture, we can work together amidst tremendous diversity.

If we take the truths of this passage and apply it to cross-cultural ministry partnerships, we can also begin to consider on the front end of things what is most critical. We all believe that Jesus was God's only begotten Son, sent to atone for the sins of humankind. We believe all who come to him in faith will have their sins forgiven and will be redeemed. We see in John 17 that unity is necessary for the world to know that God sent Jesus. Within the scope of this bigger picture we can commit up front that our cross-cultural ministry partnerships will reflect unity so the witness of Christ will not be marred. There are a number of big picture truths we can agree on in the initial stages of forming cross-cultural partnerships. As Wycliffe members covenant up front to stay focused on the overarching doctrinal truths, so partners can agree to stay focused on core issues so they do not get dragged off course while arguing over lesser things. *Are you focusing on the bigger issues of modeling unity and love?*

3. Take the extra steps and invest the time and creativity necessary to meet not only your own needs and requirements but those of your partner as well. Verses 3-4: "Do nothing from selfishness or empty conceit, but with humility of mind regard one another as more important than yourselves; do not merely look out for your own personal interests, but also for the interests of others."

This issue is such an important litmus test for us to know if we are doing ministry under the lordship of Christ or for less noble reasons. Jesus does not just care what we accomplish in life through our own cross-cultural ministry. He is not just outcome-based in his evaluation of our work. He cares deeply about the process, the way in which we go about our ministries, and the effect we are having on others along the way. Sometimes outcome-based goals might be met but the overall toll on the kingdom of God is worse than before the partnership began because of harsh words, hurt feelings, and lingering resentment and bitterness. It takes humility to be able to look past our own needs and recognize the needs of others. It takes humility to realize we are not the center of the universe and our goals are not the most important ones on the planet. When it comes to partnership and money, it means Majority World partners taking the necessary though possibly annoying and irritating steps to help ensure that their Western partners do not violate laws and incur negative corporate or legal consequences. It also means wealthier partners considering and creatively utilizing resources within their power to help less affluent partners meet their societal obligations and requirements so they do not experience loss of face. If we are doing partnership under the lordship of Christ, we have no other option but to invest the extra time, energy and resources necessary to meet our partner's needs as well as our own. *Are you making sure that your partner's needs as well as your own are being met?*

4. Set aside your legitimate power and do not pick it up again. Verses 5-8: "Have this attitude in yourselves which was also in Christ Jesus, who, although He existed in the form of God, did not regard equality with God a thing to be grasped, but emptied Himself, taking the form of a bond-servant, and being made in the likeness of men. Being found in appearance as a man, He humbled Himself by becoming obedient to the point of death, even death on a cross."

Jesus models how a high power, highly resourced partner should act in ministry. He could have laid claim to all kinds of rights, but he did not. At times this meant he was extremely vulnerable, yet he stayed his course. For highly resourced partners, it means we see ourselves as equals and we do not use money to get our way. Power is a funny thing. Money is power but so too are unjust moments of suffering from the past like harm from colonialism or paternalism. Both sides of a partnership have access to power, though the actual type may vary. Are we willing to follow the example of Jesus and set power aside? Are we willing to relinquish power when we feel threatened or when we want our way? Are we willing to trust our heavenly Father for the outcome? It is often necessary to forgive and remember for change to occur. But remembering is not the same as using past hurts to intimidate others. This passage has extreme implications for how partners can come together for the good of the kingdom despite incredible differences. *Are you setting aside legitimate power to be a servant in the partnership?*

5. Know that God will reward humility and obedience. Verses 9-11: "For this reason also, God highly exalted Him, and bestowed on Him, the name which is above every name, so that at the name of Jesus EVERY KNEE WILL BOW, of those who are in heaven and on earth and under the earth, and that every tongue confess that Jesus Christ is Lord, to the glory of God the Father."

Faith is not a simple, easy thing. True faith grows through trials and testing. Yet we see from this passage that God highly exalted Jesus because of his humility and obedience. Often when we choose not to be humble and obedient, it is because we doubt God will truly reward us. We in essence go about getting the reward ourselves. Do we want to take rewards by pushing and making things happen through our own strength? Or do we want the profound and utter privilege of experiencing God working in and among us? Do we want to see God do great things? If so, we need to walk in faith, trusting and knowing that God will reward a path of humility and obedience. We see this time and again in Scripture, but in our competitive and ambitious world we frequently need to be reminded of this reality. *Are you walking humbly, trusting that God will reward your obedience?*

6. **Expect that partnering well will take a lot of work, and that is okay.** Verses 12-13: "So then, my beloved, just as you have always obeyed, not as in my presence only, but now much more in my absence, work out your salvation with fear and trembling; for it is God who is at work in you, both to will and to work for His good pleasure."

Sometimes we get deceived and think something is only of God if it comes together easily. Sometimes that is true. Because of the grace of God, some things do seem effortless. However, the lordship of Christ is often not modeled through effortlessness. The lordship of Christ is often modeled through intentionality, consistency, faithfulness, patience and long-suffering. Doing cross-cultural ministry partnerships in a way that will truly reflect the lordship of Christ will take work—often hard work! But with this reality God provides such an awe-inspiring promise. He does not leave us to work it out in our own efforts. Some translations say he will work in you both to make you willing and able to do his good pleasure. We are not alone in this effort. He does not cast us aside to figure it out and work it out ourselves. He works amidst us and empowers us to do his will. But this will not happen if we do not commit ourselves to working hard. *Are you doing the hard work to ensure your partnership is effective and fruitful?*

7. *Know that if you choose to work in respectful and loving ways, you will shine forth with the powerful radiance of the glory of God.* Verses 15-16: "Do all things without grumbling or disputing; so that you will prove yourselves to be blameless and innocent, children of God above reproach in the midst of a crooked and perverse generation, among whom you appear as lights in the world,

holding fast the word of life, so that in the day of Christ I will have reason to glory because I did not run in vain nor toil in vain."

My husband and I have not been able to have children. However, I am fascinated as I watch others parent and as I watch children interact. Most of the time I deeply enjoy being with my own nieces and nephews. I truly treasure time together because I think they are such great people. The only time this is not the case is when they are bickering with one another. It drives me crazy, it drives their parents crazy, and I have a feeling it irritates God. If we know that reality as adults, why do we not see the parallel reality when we fight and argue with one another? Perhaps it is because fighting and arguing is so much the norm for humanity that when we opt to live differently, the world turns its head and watches. In a world filled with strife and terrorism and culture wars, God indicates that if we choose to live differently, our witness for him will shine with profound intensity.

Do we want God himself to be seen in our cross-cultural ministry partnerships? As we come to the table with different opinions and different ways of working, are we willing to surrender everything we bring to a greater One, whose wisdom and character and obedience have proven to be trustworthy? Are we willing to have a new vision for cross-cultural ministry partnerships? Are we willing to let Christ be Lord of how we work with one another? If the answer is yes, Philippians 2:1-16 seems to provide a good picture of what it will look like and the powerful outcomes it will produce. *Are you speaking in respectful ways and turning away from the sin of grumbling?*

THE AMAZING POSSIBILITY

I dream of a day when Philippians 2:1-16 is not the exception but rather the norm for cross-cultural ministry partnerships. I dream of the day when we choose not to compartmentalize our theology and how we do ministry, but rather, our theology informs and transforms how we work with one another. I dream of a day, and I can see it in my heart, when the world stops and takes notice of what is happening in our cross-cultural ministry partnerships. I dream of the day when world leaders come to Christians to see how they can get along better because the global church is modeling this so very beautifully. I do not believe it is a pipe dream. It is a promise right here in Scripture that we can choose to live out if we desire these outcomes.

If we do not want to allow Christ to be Lord of our cross-cultural partnerships, I am afraid the outcome will be much different. If we reject the truths of this passage our witness will be bleak. I think some things will happen but most likely there will be more harm than good. Gains in one area will produce profound dysfunction and damage in other areas. The chasm of differences will be too great to weather.

I believe we are on the cusp of seeing something spectacular happen in global missions. We are about to see the greatest advancement of the gospel ever before witnessed in the world. I see God's global church positioned with unparalleled resources in technology, theological training, willing laborers and financial resources. The missing ingredients—grace and love—will come in abundance as we submit it all to the lordship of Christ for his glory and for his purposes. There we will find what we have been lacking![1]

Finding Grace in the Big Picture

I wish I could say that I never grow weary in cross-cultural partnerships. I would like to say that I'm always godly and I always instinctively believe the best in people. I wish I never got frustrated, irritated or annoyed when things did not turn out as I thought they should. This is not true though. Some of the insights and lessons shared in this book have come out of my own mistakes, my own misunderstandings, and at times my own broken relationships. I am embarrassed by some of the failures I have had in ministry. I wish at times that I could turn back the clock and have a "do-over." But God does not give us that option. Instead he asks that we learn from our mistakes and mature. That is what growing in cultural intelligence is all about.

Finding Help in the Big Picture

To be honest, as I grow as a Christian what keeps me going is remembering the "big picture." The big picture in cross-cultural partnerships is the truth of John 17:20-26. It is not about which partner gets his or her way. It is about working in a way that models unity so the witness of Christ is not hindered in the world. It is remembering the amazing truth of Revelation 5:9-10. Christ, through his very blood, purchased people from every tongue and tribe and nation. Our eternal destiny is to be with all these brothers and sisters from so many different races and nationalities. We will be "about kingdom business" for all eternity. Perhaps experiences now are just a test run, a chance to learn skills and develop character so God's eternal plans can be established?

The message in the twelfth and thirteenth chapters of the book of Romans comes to mind. We are first all members of one body. The twelfth chapter of 1 Corinthians unpacks what that means. We are dependent on one another. We are called to care about each part of the body of Christ. Success is not legitimate if it is at the expense, harm or detriment to any member of that body. That is our first identity, and it needs to be our first priority. It is not about meeting our own objectives, organizational ends or outcomes. It is deeper than that. It is about working in a way that enables every member or "partner" to flourish as we seek to reach important goals together. Our next priority is taking care to honor and meet governmental requirements. The reason and importance for this is outlined in the thirteenth chapter of Romans. It is not an either-or equation but a both/and equation. It is not about either caring about people or adhering to government regulations. We are called to do both.

If the going gets tough, we are not left to work this out in our own strength. We have the incredible prayer that Christ taught all his followers. He exhorts us to pray that "thy will be done on earth as it is in heaven." What is the will of the One we serve? It is that our actions and behavior would model the values of heaven. We do not have this capacity within ourselves but we can pray for it, and we are urged by Christ to pray. The big picture is that God has a spectacular plan for all people and at this time we only see a tiny glimpse of it. He is doing something great in the world, and if we are willing to follow him, we get the amazing privilege of having a small part in it.

Transforming Partnership

The Coalition on the Support of Indigenous Ministries (COSIM) coordinates a conference each year so people who want to become better cross-cultural partners can come and learn from one another. One year Rev. Moses Swamidas from Bible Faith Mission shared his testimony. Moses was a Dalit. He was raised in South Asia to think of himself as worthless, an untouchable. As a child as he walked down the street, if even his shadow fell on another, the person of a different caste would be considered unclean and would need to go home immediately and shower. These experiences and many more like them over time left Moses feeling unlovable and wholly worthless. But Moses put his faith in Christ, and he decided to start reaching out to those around him to help ease his peoples' suffering.

Moses began evangelizing, and many came to faith in Christ as a result of his ministry. He also formed all kinds of ministry programs so children would be able to have some of their most basic needs met and have an opportunity to go to school. A Western partner learned about this ministry in its initial phases. He arranged a meeting and started to form a relationship with Moses. Sometimes the Western partner came with his friends from abroad. Although happy at the thought of getting support for this work, Moses was ill at ease. He was so ashamed of the dark color of his skin and the fact that he was of such a low and unvalued caste. When his overseas partners would visit his home, Moses said he could never join them at the table. He felt wholly inadequate and unworthy to even share a meal with them. So he always arranged to eat on the floor or at another time. He could not figure out why these high-status white people cared about what he was doing; for his own people. No one else in the world ever seemed to care, why did they?

As Moses told the story, he explained that little by little his thoughts and opinions about himself began to change. As these Western partners invested in him and his ministry, he realized that there must be something worthwhile about who he was and what he was doing. The funding helped him to reach far more people for Christ, yet these Western partners always seemed to care about *him*. And they seemed to value and respect *him*. Over time he became more secure and more courageous. After a number of years he began joining them in laughter and fellowship at the same table over meals. He no longer felt like an unlovable or unworthy person.

Moses said, "I now go to the Supreme Court in my country, and I fight for my people. I fight for their rights. I fight for their dignity. I fight that they might have opportunities to grow and develop wholly as God desires. I have this sense of confidence, and I know my people are worthwhile because my Western partners showed me through their love and care and belief in me over the years that I was called by God and I could make a difference in the world. I am bold now. I know I am loved by God. I know he will do great things through me. I am no longer ashamed. I am just as valuable as anyone else because I am a child of God!"

WE NEED EACH OTHER

In this story Moses needed his partners to be able to grow and develop into the fullness of the person God had made him to be. But the need is not one-sided. I recently talked with a friend who is a mission pastor of a large church in the United States. A ministry partner from East Asia was the guest speaker at a recent mission festival held at the church. I know the guest speaker, and she is an exceptional human being.

When I inquired about how it went my friend said, "In every single service, she used different stories about how God's hand is working miraculously in the lives of so many people in Asia. Although she spoke at multiple services over the course of the weekend, she never repeated any stories! It was as though there was no end to what God was doing in that part of the world. She totally challenged all of our neat little categories about how God works. The staff talked after she left, and we realized that there is a whole different level of intimacy with God and fruitfulness that we have never even begun to experience. She stayed at my house and each morning I heard her in the other room worshipping at 5 a.m.!"

We both chuckled and shook our heads as my friend recounted the experience. It was a nervous laughter, the type that erupts when we feel embarrassed or a bit undone. How can we grow to maturity in Christ if we do not work together? How will we ever overcome selfishness and sinfulness if all we compare ourselves with are those who look and act just like us? We partner and work with our brothers and sisters around the world for reasons far deeper than any specific ministry outcome or objective. We partner cross-culturally because in the deepest recesses of our soul and being we need one another to become the people that God created us to be!

LEARNING FROM THE
"SISTER CHURCH" PARTNERSHIP

I introduced this book with a story about a partnership between an American church and a congregation in Eastern Europe. I wish the mistakes made in that partnership were rare. However, this story seems to embody so many of the mistakes and misunderstandings I have heard time and again in various parts of the world. Perhaps after reading through this book, you can now see more clearly the reasons why it happened. I believe it serves as a helpful case study for deeper learning that you can use individually or with team members or partners.

PREPARATION

Read through the story in the introduction again (pp. 22-27).

CORE CULTURAL CONCEPTS

• How did the American church's individualistic worldview and

Alex's collectivistic worldview affect expectations about partnership? What makes each of these perspectives legitimate (pp. 33-43)?

- What steps might Ed have taken prior to his visit to Eastern Europe that might have helped to alleviate or lessen the chance of this misunderstanding occurring?

- During Ed's visit, how did a misunderstanding about high and low context communication contribute to the problem (pp. 47-48)?

- Think of your own cross-cultural partnerships. What nonverbal messages are you sending that might confuse your cross-cultural partner? Do you think your cross-cultural partner feels comfortable telling you about mixed messages? Why or why not? How might understanding status issues enable you to create ways for him or her to convey this type of information (pp. 45-47)?

- In this story how did the use of the word "sister" impact expectations (pp. 40-42)? Why might these expectations be legitimate if we choose to use family nomenclature?

UPROOTING THE HARMFUL

- How did Alex "make meaning" in this situation (pp. 69-76)? Did the way he made meaning help or hurt him? Why?

- Do you see any paternalistic behaviors or attitudes in the American church (pp. 78-81)?

- Are there any paternalistic behaviors or attitudes in your cross-cultural partnership? What culturally appropriate avenues could be developed that would enable your partner to tell you if this was indeed the case?

- How might an understanding of John Rowell's metaphor have led to a better outcome when Ed, the senior pastor, presented the proposal to the American church's elder board (p. 83)?

- In light of the behaviors and circumstances in the Eastern European church, would sharing funds for a building project foster unhealthy dependency? Why or why not? In this post-communist culture, how might a sharing of funds by the American church have fostered a deeper and richer witness of Christ in this community (pp. 87-93)?

PARTNERING IN BETTER WAYS

- In what ways was Ed holding the Eastern European congregation to a higher level of accountability than he was requiring of himself (pp. 105-7)?

- In what ways was Ed exporting how things should be done without taking care to understand how processes worked in that Eastern European context (pp. 112-19)?

- What important contributions are being brought to your cross-cultural ministry partnership besides money (pp. 125-27)?

- Have you designed accountability structures that foster mutuality so accountability goes in both directions (pp. 127-31)?

- What is a ministry or church's obligation to consider its own capacity in terms of giving and what it promises during overseas visits? What is the outcome if a church's leaders promise things that cannot be delivered?

REDEEMING CONFLICT

- What have you learned about conflict and about yourself from this story?

- What processes have you formed for your partnership to ensure that you will manage future conflicts in ways that might strengthen instead of destroy your cross-cultural relationships (pp. 147-60)?

GRACE IN THE BIG PICTURE

- How might having a focus on the big picture have influenced the decision of the American church about whether to help in funding the new church building in Eastern Europe (pp. 189-91)?

- How might an understanding of the big picture have helped Alex to work through his anger and hurt over the behavior of his "sister church" partner (pp. 191-93)?

- How will an understanding of the big picture impact how you will choose to relate with your cross-cultural partners?

FACILITATING A CULTURE
OF FISCAL INTEGRITY

I see ministry leaders making a common mistake when it comes to the topic of fiscal integrity. Often they think if they lecture about its importance or include it in written documentation about a partnership, fiscal integrity will magically materialize. It is not that easy though. Only as we engage in true dialogue will we be able to form a lasting culture of fiscal integrity.

When I mention dialoguing about this issue, some ministry leaders seem squeamish. They want fiscal integrity but they seem afraid to talk about it. Perhaps this is a remnant of the colonial period. Western partners do not want to be perceived as being controlling or neo-colonialistic. However, the core reality each ministry faces is that if there is not a culture of fiscal integrity, the partnership will likely come unglued. For this reason, it is helpful to ask questions and get people talking about this issue sooner rather than later. Here are some issues that are necessary to consider if we want to help jumpstart the dialogue.

1. PICK THE FACILITATOR WITH CARE

People will only speak openly if they feel safe. For true dialogue to take place, the facilitator needs to be someone they trust. This trust can come from two factors. First, the person should be known and respected by those engaged in the dialogue as someone who is faithful and a good steward of funds, and who lives this out both explicitly and implicitly. Second, the person needs to be a gentle-natured outsider with experience in the area and without the implicit baggage that will cause people not to listen. What constitutes implicit baggage will vary from culture to culture. If people generally dislike Americans and feel they are wasteful and materialistic, it is probable best not to have an American leading the dialogue! However, if the American is perceived as being an expert in the area and he or she is kind and warm natured, true dialogue will likely result. A key to picking the right facilitator is to ask the participants which people they think would be best to lead the discussion.

2. ALLOW ADEQUATE TIME

True dialogue is something that cannot be rushed. This process will work best if it is done in a retreat setting over the course of a day or two, or if it is done in blocks of time over the course of a few months. Please do not think you can foster genuine dialogue and cover all the significant issues in an hour or two. Brevity in dialogue will not make a significant impact on the organizational culture.

3. ASK ENGAGING QUESTIONS

Here is just a sample to get you thinking of the types of questions that might work best. I have broken the list into different segments. It is best to take a break between sections so people stay fresh and alert.

Connecting with People's Experiences and Feelings

a. Have you seen cases where people have stolen from government funds, company funds or ministries in your country? What stories can you share from the things you have seen or heard personally or in the news?

b. What impact have these types of sin or corruption had on your culture? Who are the people you see suffering the most?

c. How have these acts influenced how you think and how you see the world?

d. How do you think people view funds that come from abroad versus funds that are raised for ministry from within this community or country?

e. What will happen to our ministry if funds get stolen or misused?

f. How does theft or misuse of finances affect people's personal relationships?

g. How will your life be affected if someone else takes and misuses funds that are set aside for this ministry?

h. How are the gospel and the witness of Christ affected when funds are stolen or misused in ministry?

Connecting with God and His Word

a. How do you think God feels about funds being taken from a ministry and used for other purposes?

b. Are there times you think it is OK and times it is not OK? What makes the difference?

c. Are there Scripture passages that address the use or misuse of funds? (Take time to look at each one closely.)

d. What does this mean for us as believers in ministry?

Uncovering Vulnerable Areas

a. In our context and ministry, what areas are most vulnerable?

b. How might fraud occur? (Brainstorm ideas.)

Conextualizing Processes

a. What processes might lessen temptation for people?

b. In light of our limited resources and staffing, what actions can we take to protect our ministry from suffering from this sin?

c. What should we do when someone is caught stealing funds from this ministry?

d. What are the obstacles, the practical roadblocks you see, to addressing theft or misuse of funds in this ministry?

e. What ideas might help you get around these roadblocks?

4. ROLE PLAY

Set aside time to create and practice skits, or role play scenarios that could arise. Let people practice different scenarios until you sense a comfort level and confidence that they could truly act on these ideas.

5. STAY FOCUSED

Organizational culture is built and fashioned by what leaders and administrators regularly pay attention to. How will this focus be built into your regular structures and meetings to be sure you remember and foster a culture of fiscal integrity? Who will make sure this happens? How will you continue to remember the things you have discussed?

6. CONCLUSION

Conclude by reinforcing what the true motivation needs to be in any effort to create a culture of fiscal integrity: a love for God, a love for people, the desire for the witness of Christ not to be marred, and a desire for the ministry to flourish and touch more lives.

This type of list should give you a good start. Your cross-cultural partners or others involved in the ministry might have additional questions and ideas that would be good to add. If we choose the path of dialogue, we have a greater chance of building a culture of fiscal integrity that will stand the test of time.

RECOMMENDATIONS FOR FURTHER READING

CROSS-CULTURAL PARTNERSHIP

There are a growing number of books dealing with cross-cultural partnerships. I think two are especially helpful.

Making Your Partnership Work by Daniel Rickett

Well Connected: Releasing Power, Restoring Hope Through Kingdom Partnerships by Phill Butler

CROSS-CULTURAL MINISTRY

It is difficult to be effective in cross-cultural ministry if we harbor paternalistic attitudes, if we do not understand the most basic dimensions of culture, if we have not thought through the issue of conflict and if we are unwilling to keep a big-picture focus. For that reason I highly recommend the following books.

Cross-Cultural Servanthood: Serving the World in Christlike Humility by Duane Elmer

Cross-Cultural Connections: Stepping Out and Fitting In Around the World by Duane Elmer

Cross-Cultural Conflict: Building Relationships for More Effective Ministry by Duane Elmer

Leading Cross-Culturally: Covenant Relationships for Effective Christian Leadership by Sherwood Lingenfelter

THE DEPENDENCY AND GIVING DEBATE

When it comes to issues such as giving, power, inequality and unhealthy financial dependency, these books are a great starting place to begin to understand the complexities.

To Give or Not to Give: Rethinking Dependency, Restoring Generosity and Redefining Sustainability by John Rowell

When Charity Destroys Dignity: Overcoming Unhealthy Dependency in the Christian Movement by Glenn Schwartz

Rich Christians in an Age of Hunger: Moving from Affluence to Generosity by Ronald Sider

Missions and Money by Jonathon Bonk

CULTURE AND MONEY

An exceptional book is titled *African Friends and Money Matters* by David Maranz. He analyzes the differences in how Africans and Western missionaries view resources. I have found his insights helpful and applicable in a number of collective cultures in many different parts of the world.

CULTURAL RESEARCH

An insightful journal for cross-cultural research is *The International Journal for Intercultural Relations*. Key social science authors and researchers are Geert Hofstede, Edward Hall, Craig Storti,

William Gudykunst and Stella Ting-Toomey. If you do a Google search with their names you will find all kinds of interesting books and journal articles. You can then glean their bibliographies for even more resources.

One of the reasons we are not learning more quickly is because we limit our readings to those who have gone through a master of divinity program at a leading seminary. I like to glean findings from social science research and then test it against Scripture. If the principles align, I then view it as general revelation and common grace, which God has provided for us to live and work more effectively. I also like to simply talk and learn from partners. Often we can learn volumes if we just listen.

Notes

Introduction: Partnership, Money and Cultural Intelligence

[1]In a presentation at the COSIM (Coalition on the Support of Indigenous Ministries) Conference held at Wheaton Bible Church on June 10, 2007, Scott Moreau shared the statistic that in the United States from the period beginning 1998 until 2005 there was a 6900% increase in the number of churches and mission agencies claiming that partnership is now a primary method for engaging in global missions.

[2]Phill Butler's book *Well Connected: Releasing Power, Restoring Hope Through Kingdom Partnerships,* is an excellent resource for those wanting to form healthy partnerships. Another excellent and helpful resource is Daniel Rickett's book *Making Your Partnership Work.*

[3]Sherwood Lingenfelter also references this phenomenon on page 200 of his book coauthored with Bobby Gupta, *Breaking Tradition to Accomplish Vision.*

[4]Identities and locations have been altered to protect the confidentiality of those involved. This story was chosen because the mistakes that were made are not uncommon ones. They are incredibly easy to make by those who have not received a lot of training in cross-cultural ministry.

[5]Howard Gardner wrote the book *Multiple Intelligences,* which opened the door to begin researching other forms of intelligence.

[6]Daniel Golemen built upon Gardner's research as he began to uncover the issue of emotional intelligence. As he examined the implications of this concept in the real-world context in his book *Working with Emotional Intelligence,* he found that human beings could continue to grow in this area even through old age. Many findings from emotional intelligence research intersect with cultural intelligence. See Brooks Peterson's book

Cultural Intelligence: A Guide to Working with People from Other Cultures as one example.

Chapter 1: Is It "Mine" or "Ours"?

[1]Paul G. Hiebert, *Anthropological Insights for Missionaries* (Grand Rapids: Baker, 1985), p. 97.

[2]Ibid., p. 112.

[3]Geert Hofstede, *Cultures and Organizations: Software of the Mind* (London: McGraw-Hill, 1991), p. 51. The term "immediate family" includes the father, mother and their children only.

[4]Geert Hofstede and Gert Jan Hofstede, *Cultures and Organizations: Software of the Mind*, 2nd ed. (New York: McGraw-Hill, 2005), p. 75.

[5]Ibid.

[6]Ibid., p. 87.

[7]William B. Gudykunst et al., "The Influence of Cultural Individualism-Collectivism, Self Construals and Individual Values on Communicaiton Styles Across Cultures," *Human Communication Research* 22 (1996): 510-43.

[8]David Maranz, *African Friends and Money Matters* (Dallas: SIL International and the International Museum of Cultures, 2001).

[9]Ibid., p. 4.

[10]Ibid.

[11]Ibid., p. 5.

[12]Ibid., p. 69.

[13]John Watters, 2007. The hard work of authentic partnership: still learning to transition from a more member-focused to a more inclusive and partnership-focused ministry. 2007 COSIM Conference. COSIM web resources. www.cosim.info

Chapter 2: Communication and Harmony

[1]Stella Ting-Toomey and John G. Oetzel, "Cross-Cultural Face Concerns and Conflict Styles," in *Cross-Cultural and Intercultural Communication*, ed. William B. Gudykunst (Thousand Oaks, Calif.: Sage, 2003), p. 129.

[2]D. F. E. Ho, "On the Concept of Face," *American Journal of Sociology* 81 (1976): 867.

[3]For more information on this concept, read Geert Hofstede and Gert Jan Hofstede, *Cultures and Organizations: Software of the Mind*, 2nd ed. (New York: McGraw-Hill, 2005); Craig Storti, *Figuring Foreigners Out: A Practical Guide* (Yarmouth, Me.: Intercultural Press, 1999); Duane Elmer, *Cross-Cultural Connections: Stepping Out and Fitting in Around the World* (Downers Grove, Ill.: InterVarsity Press, 2002); or Sherwood G. Lingenfelter and

Marvin K. Mayers, *Ministering Cross-Culturally: An Incarnational Model for Personal Relationships* (Grand Rapids: Baker Academic, 2003).

[4]For more information about this, read the books written by Edward T. Hall (see the bibliography for a list). He was the first person to highlight the role of context and is often referred to as the father of intercultural communication.

[5]Elmer, *Cross-Cultural Connections,* p. 167.

[6]Judith E. Lingenfelter and Sherwood G. Lingenfelter,. *Teaching Cross-Culturally: An Incarnational Model for Learning and Teaching* (Grand Rapids: Baker Academic, 2003), p. 108.

[7]Robert R. Blake and Jane S. Mouton, *The Managerial Grid* (Houston: Gulf Publishing, 1964).

[8]John Rowell, *To Give or Not to Give: Rethinking Dependence, Restoring Generosity and Redefining Sustainability* (Atlanta: Authentic Publishing, 2006).

[9]Glenn Schwartz, *When Charity Destroys Dignity: Overcoming Unhealthy Dependency in the Christian Movement* (Bloomington, Ind.: AuthorHouse, 2007), p. 84.

[10]Duane Elmer, *Cross-Cultural Servanthood: Serving the World in Christlike Humility* (Downers Grove, Ill.: InterVarsity Press, 2006), p. 141.

[11]K. P. Yohannan, *Revolution in World Missions* (Carrolton, Tex.: GFA, 2004), p. 44.

Chapter 3: Other Confusing Issues

[1]Craig Storti, *Figuring Foreigners Out: A Practical Guide* (Yarmouth, Me.: Intercultural Press, 1999), p. 38.

[2]Ibid., pp. 38-39.

[3]Fons Trompenaars and Charles Hampden-Turner, *Riding the Waves of Culture: Understanding Diversity in Global Business,* 2nd ed. (New York: McGraw-Hill, 1998), pp. 31-32.

[4]Nancy J. Adler, *International Dimensions of Organizational Behavior* (Belmont, Calif.: Wadsworth, 1986), p. 87.

[5]Geert Hofstede and Gert Jan Hofstede, *Cultures and Organizations: Software of the Mind,* 2nd ed. (New York: McGraw-Hill, 2005), p. 163.

[6]Ibid., p. 167.

[7]Ibid., p. 171.

[8]Ibid., p. 176.

[9]Ibid., p. 257.

[10]Edward T. Hall, *The Dance of Life: The Other Dimension of Time* (Garden City, N.Y.: Anchor Press, 1983), p. 48.

[11]Edward T. Hall, *The Silent Language* (Westport, Conn.: Greenwood Press, 1959), p. 19.

[12]Storti, *Figuring Foreigners Out,* p. 55.

[13]Hall, *The Dance of Life,* p. 46.

[14]Ibid., p. 50.

[15]Storti, *Figuring Foreigners Out,* p. 55.

[16]Hall, *The Dance of Life,* p. 52.

[17]Ibid., p. 50.

[18]Ibid., p. 53.

Chapter 4: The Path to Premature Judgments

[1]Patricia Cranton, *Understanding and Promoting Transformative Learning: A Guide for Educators of Adults,* 2nd ed. (San Francisco: John Wiley & Sons, 2006), p. 28. This area of meaning making is foundational in transformative learning theory developed by Jack Mezirow.

[2]Duane Elmer, IMCO Conference, Saskatchewan, Canada, 2007; and chapter 3 of *Cross-Cultural Connections: Stepping Out and Fitting in Around the World* (Downers Grove, Ill.: InterVarsity Press, 2002).

[3]I Googled "negative attribution theory," expecting to find all kinds of references to it. However, I have not found any other references to this phrase. I think it is something that Duane coined over the years as he considered other theories and situations he was encountering throughout the world. For this reason, I think he should be noted or given credit for this "spin" on attribution theory.

[4]Ibid., 2007.

[5]Raymond S. Nickerson, "Confirmation Bias: A Ubiquitous Phenomenon in Many Guises," *Review of General Psychology* 2, no. 2 (1998): 175.

[6]Ibid., pp. 175-76.

[7]Ibid., p. 181.

[8]Ibid., p. 175.

[9]Daniel T. Gilbert, Brett W. Pelham and Douglas S. Krull, "On Cognitive Busyness When Person Perceivers Meet Persons Perceived," *Journal of Personality and Social Psychology* 54, no. 5 (1988): 733.

[10]Daniel Gilbert and Patrick Malone, "The Correspondence Bias," *Psychological Bulletin* 117, no. 1 (1995): 21.

[11]C. S. Lewis, *The Weight of Glory* (New York: Touchstone, 1975), p. 135.

[12]Gilbert and Malone, "Correspondence Bias," p. 21.

[13]J. N. Bassili and M. C. Smith, "On the Spontaneity of Trait Attribution: Converging Evidence for the Role of Cognitive Strategy," *Journal of Personality and Social Psychology* 50 (1986): 239.

[14]Terence Mitchell and Stephen Green, "Attribution Theory: Managerial Perceptions of the Poor Performing Subordinate," in John B. Miner, *Organizational Behavior 1: Essential Theories of Motivation and Leadership* (Armonk, N.Y.: M. E. Sharpe, 2005), p. 189.

[15]Ibid.

[16]Philip E. Tetlock, "Accountability: A Social Check on the Fundamental Attribution Error," *Social Psychology Quarterly* 48, no. 3 (1985): 227.

[17]Nickerson, "Confirmation Bias," p. 211.

[18]Ibid., p. 200.

[19]Gilbert et al., "On Cognitive Busyness," p. 735.

Chapter 5: Paternalism Couched as Accountability

[1]Galatians 3:7, "Therefore, be sure that it is those who are of faith who are the sons of Abraham."

[2]1 Timothy 1:2, "to Timothy, my true child in the faith."

[3]Ed Wood and Les Willis, "Paternalism, Accountability, Responsibility and Transparency," IMCO Conference. Saskatchewan, Canada, 2007.

[4]Ibid.

[5]*The New Merriam-Webster Dictionary* (Springfield, Mass.: Merriam-Webster, 1989), p. 534.

[6]K. P. Yohannan, *Revolution in World Missions* (Carrolton, Tex.: GFA Books, 2004), p. 152.

[7]Nancy J. Adler, *International Dimensions of Organizational Behavior* (Belmont, Calif.: Wadsworth, 1986), pp. 11-12.

[8]Duane Elmer, *Cross-Cultural Servanthood: Serving the World in Christlike Humility* (Downers Grove, Ill.: InterVarsity Press, 2006), p. 17

[9]Ibid., p. 20.

[10]Yohannan, *Revolution in World Missions*, p. 88.

[11]Robert Rosenthal, *On the Social Psychology of the Self-Fulfilling Prophecy: Further Evidence for the Pygmalion Effects* (New York: MSS Modular Publications, 1974); Robert Rosenthal, "Interpersonal Expectance Effects: A 30-year Perspective," *Current Directions in Psychological Science* 3, no. 6 (1994): 176-79; Robert Rosenthal and Lenore Jacobson, *Pygmalion in the Classroom: Teacher Expectation and Pupils' Intellectual Development* (New York: Holt, Rinehart & Winston, 1968).

[12]John Rowell, *To Give or Not to Give: Rethinking Dependence, Restoring Generosity and Redefining Sustainability* (Atlanta: Authentic Publishing, 2006).

[13]Ibid., pp. 18-19.

[14]Peter M. Senge, foreword in David Bohm, *On Dialogue* (London: Routledge, 1999), p. x.

Chapter 6: Common Unintended Consequences

[1]John Rowell, *To Give or Not to Give: Rethinking Dependence, Restoring Generosity and Redefining Sustainability* (Atlanta: Authentic Publishing, 2006).

[2]Glenn Schwartz, *When Charity Destroys Dignity: Overcoming Unhealthy Dependency in the Christian Movement* (Bloomington, Ind.: AuthorHouse, 2007).

[3]Ibid., p. 14.

[4]Ibid., p. 42.

[5]Ibid., p. 111.

[6]Ibid., p. 240.

[7]Mary Lederleitner, "Funding Kingdom Work by Empowering Indigenous Organizations: Lessons Learned in Wycliffe International's Matching Funds Experiment," *Evangelical Missions Quarterly*, July 2009.

[8]Schwartz, *When Charity Destroys Dignity*, p. 37.

[9]Rowell, *To Give or Not to Give*.

[10]Langdon Gilkey, *Shantung Compound* (New York: HarperCollins, 1966).

[11]Ibid., p. 96.

[12]Ibid., p. 100.

[13]Ibid., p. 102.

[14]Ibid., p. 105.

[15]Sherwood G. Lingenfelter, Plenary Sessions, COSIM Conference, 2007. COSIM web resources. www.cosim.info. For more information about "default culture," read Sherwood Lingenfelter's book *Leading Cross-Culturally: Covenant Relationships for Effective Christian Leadership* (Grand Rapids: Baker Academic, 2008).

[16]Daniel Goleman, *Working with Emotional Intelligence* (New York: Bantam Books, 1998).

[17]Ronald J. Sider, *Rich Christians in an Age of Hunger: Moving from Affluence to Generosity* (Nashville: Thomas Nelson, 2005)

Chapter 7: Biblical Foundations for Accountability

[1]This statistic is from page 12 of Larry Burkett's book *Budget Counselor Training Course Textbook* (Gainsville, Ga.: Crown Financial Ministries, 2003).

[2]The first time I fully grasped the concept that this tree in the Garden was God's "donor-designated resource" was in a very tiny pamphlet. I have no idea who wrote it. I think it might have been produced by TEAM, but I am not sure. It was a short little booklet written by a missionary who had extensive overseas experience. I apologize to that writer for not being able to cite his name and give him full credit at this time.

Chapter 8: Contexualizing Accounting Processes

[1]C.K. Prahalad and Kenneth Lieberthal, "The End of Corporate Imperialism," *Harvard Business Review* 81, no. 8 (2003): 116.

[2]Mary Lederleitner, "The Theology of Internal Controls," *Evangelical Missions Quarterly* 40, no. 4 (2006): 521.

[3]E. Dale Berkey and Doug Brendel, *The Disappearing Donor* (Akron, Ohio: Berkey Brendel Sheline, 2005), p. 3.

[4]Ibid., p. 22.

Chapter 9: Fostering Dignity and Mutuality

[1]John Watters, "The Hard Work of Authentic Partnership: Still Learning to Transition from a More Member-Focused to a More Inclusive and Partnership-focused Ministry." COSIM Conference, 2007. COSIM web resources .www.cosim.info.

[2]Ibid.

[3]Daniel Rickett, *Making Your Partnership Work* (Enumclaw, Wash.: WinePress Publishing, 2002), p. 39.

[4]Stan Nussbaum, *American Cultural Baggage: How to Recognize and Deal with It* (Maryknoll, N.Y.: Orbis, 2005), p. 11.

[5]John Rowell, *To Give or Not to Give: Rethinking Dependence, Restoring Generosity and Redefining Sustainability* (Atlanta: Authentic Publishing, 2006), p. 157.

[6]David Maranz, *African Friends and Money Matters* (Dallas: SIL International and the International Museum of Cultures, 2001).

[7]Ibid., p. 39.

[8]Daniel Goleman, *Working with Emotional Intelligence* (New York: Bantam Books, 1998), pp. 251-53.

[9]David Bohm, *On Dialogue* (New York: Routledge, 1996), p. 5.

[10]Goleman, *Working with Emotional Intelligence*, pp. 251-53.

[11]Raymond G. Helmick, S.J., and Rodney L. Peterson, eds., *Forgiveness and Reconciliation* (Philadelphia: Templeton Foundation Press, 2001).

[12]John Paul Lederach, "Five Qualities of Practice in Support of Reconciliation Process," in *Forgiveness and Reconciliation*, ed. Raymond G. Helmick, S.J., and Rodney L. Peterson (Philadelphia: Templeton Foundation Press, 2001), p. 201.

[13]Anthony Da Silva, S.J., "Through Nonviolence to Truth: Ghandi's Vision of Reconciliation," in *Forgiveness and Reconciliation*, ed. Raymond G Helmick, S.J., and Rodney L. Peterson (Philadelphia: Templeton Foundation Press, 2001), p. 313.

[14]David W. Augsburger, *Conflict Mediation Across Cultures* (Louisville: Westminster/John Knox Press, 1992), p. 259.

[15]Helmick and Peterson, *Forgiveness and Reconciliation*, p. xxvii.

[16]See the International Forgiveness Institute at www.forgiveness-institute .org.

Chapter 10: Building Capacity and Sustainability

[1]Howie Brant, 2008. Personal discussion and email communication.

[2]I do not know the original source for this parable.

[3]Presentations at the 2007 COSIM Conference titled "Breaking Tradition to Accomplish Vision" provide excellent resources for those interested in this topic. Especially helpful are the presentations given by John Watters, Bobby Gupta and Sherwood Lingenfelter. They can be accessed at www.cosim.info.

[4]Bryant L. Myers, *Walking with the Poor: Principles and Practices of Transformational Development* (Maryknoll, N.Y.: Orbis, 2007), pp. 174-79.

[5]Jane M. Watkins and Bernard J. Mohr, *Appreciative Inquiry: Change at the Speed of Imagination* (San Francisco: Jossey-Bass/Pfeiffer, 2001).

[6]Ibid.

[7]Myers, *Walking with the Poor*, pp. 178-79.

[8]Glenn Schwartz, *When Charity Destroys Dignity: Overcoming Unhealthy Dependency in the Christian Movement* (Bloomington, Ind.: AuthorHouse, 2007), p. 13.

[9]Myers, *Walking with the Poor*, p. 181.

Chapter 11: Choosing Your Method Carefully

[1]Sherwood G. Lingenfelter, 2007 Plenary Sessions, COSIM Conference. COSIM web resources. www.cosim.info. For more information about "default culture," read Sherwood Lingenfelter's book *Leading Cross-Culturally: Covenant Relationships for Effective Christian Leadership* (Grand Rapids: Baker Academic, 2008).

[2]Frank Dubinskas, "The Cultural Roots of Discord," in *Hidden Conflict in Organizations*, ed. Deborah M. Kolb and Jean M. Bartunek (Newbury Park, Calif.: Sage, 1992), pp. 187-88.

[3]Stella Ting-Toomey and John G. Oetzel, "Cross-Cultural Face Concerns and Conflict Styles," in *Cross-Cultural and Intercultural Communication*, ed. William B. Gudykunst (Thousand Oaks, Calif.: Sage, 2003), p. 138.

[4]Ibid., p. 139.

[5]Ibid.

[6]Galatians 3:19-20; Exodus 32:30-32; Numbers 12:6-8.

[7]Mark Davidheiser, "Culture and Mediation: A Contemporary Processual

Analysis from Southwestern Gambia," *International Journal of Intercultural Relations* 29 (2005): 713-38.

[8]Mary Lederleitner, "A Different Approach: Wycliffe's Work in Latin America. How Convictions Can Be Catalytic for Fruitful Cross-Cultural Partnerships," *Evangelical Missions Quarterly,* January 2010. This article outlines the actions taken by David Brooks and Jose de Dios to better cross-cultural partnerships in Latin America.

[9]David W. Augsburger, *Conflict Mediation Across Cultures* (Louisville: Westminster/John Knox Press, 1992), p. 78.

[10]Ibid.

[11]Stella Ting-Toomey, "Toward a Theory of Conflict and Culture," in *Communication, Culture, and Organizational Processes,* ed. William B. Gudykunst, Lea P. Stewart and Stella Ting-Toomey (Beverly Hills: Sage, 1985), p. 71.

[12]Jeff Weiss and Jonathan Hughes, "Want Collaboration? Accept and Actively Manage Conflict," *Harvard Business Review* 83, no. 3 (2005): 93.

[13]John Paul Lederach, "Five Qualities of Practice in Support of Reconciliation Process," in *Forgiveness and Reconciliation,* ed. Raymond G Helmick, S.J., and Rodney L. Peterson (Philadelphia: Templeton Foundation Press, 2001), p. 199.

[14]David W. Augsburger, *Conflict Mediation Across Cultures* (Louisville: Westminster/John Knox Press, 1992), p. 59.

[15]This story was told at the Global Leader's Meeting in November, 2007 by Michel Kemogne, the director of CABTAL (Cameroonian Association of Bible Translation and Literacy).

[16]Augsburger, *Conflict Mediation Across Cultures,* pp. 249-50.

Chapter 12: Options If Designated Funds Are Misallocated
[1]William Backus and Marie Chapian, *Telling Yourself the Truth* (Minneapolis: Bethany House, 1980). This is an interesting little book that has some good tips about how to better manage our thoughts so emotions do not get out of control.

Chapter 13: Options If Embezzlement or Fraud Occurs
[1]Howard Silverstone and Howard R. Davia, *Fraud 101,* 2nd ed. (Hoboken, N.J.: John Wiley & Sons, 2005).
[2]Ibid., pp. 6-7.

Conclusion: How to Tell If Christ Is Lord of Your Partnership
[1]Two months after writing the initial draft of this chapter I heard a similar theme in Chansamone Saiyasak's speech at the 2008 COSIM Conference.

A couple of weeks later, Alex Araujo from Partners International sent me an article written by Kang-San Tan with a similar theme. It made me wonder if the Spirit of God is moving in hearts around the globe to bring us to this same vision as the core of how we will work together in this next era of global missions.

BIBLIOGRAPHY

Adeney, Miriam. "Shalom Tourist: Loving Your Neighbor While Using Her." *Missiology* 34, no. 4 (2006): 463-76.

Adeyemo, Tokunboh, ed. *African Bible Commentary.* Nairobi: Word Alive Publishers, 2006.

Adler, Nancy J. *International Dimensions of Organizational Behavior.* Belmont, Calif.: Wadsworth, 1986.

Alcorn, Randy. *Money, Possessions, and Eternity.* Wheaton, Ill.: Tyndale House, 1989.

Arasaratnam, M. L., and Marya L. Doerfel. "Intercultural Communication Competence: Identifying Key Components from Multicultural Perspectives." *International Journal of Intercultural Relations* 29 (2005): 137-63.

Araujo, Alex, Mary Lederleitner and Werner Mischke. "To Catch the Wind: A 'New' Paradigm for Cross-Cultural Mission Partnerships." COSIM 2008, www.cosim.info.

Augsburger, David W. *Conflict Mediation Across Cultures.* Louisville: Westminster/John Knox Press, 1992.

Backus, William, and Marie Chapian. *Telling Yourself the Truth.* Minneapolis: Bethany House, 1980.

Bandura, Albert. "Self-Efficacy Mechanism in Human Agency." *American Psychologist* 37, no. 2 (1982): 122-47.

Bassili, J. N., and M. C. Smith. "On the Spontaneity of Trait Attribution: Converging Evidence for the Role of Cognitive Strategy." *Journal of Personality and Social Psychology* 50 (1986): 239-45.

Berkey, E. Dale, and Doug Brendel. *The Disappearing Donor.* Akron: Berkey Brendel Sheline, 2005.

Blake, Robert R., and Jane S. Mouton. *The Managerial Grid.* Houston: Gulf Publishing, 1964.

Bohm, David. *On Dialogue.* New York: Routledge, 1996.

Bonk, Jonathon J. *Missions and Money.* Maryknoll, N.Y.: Orbis, 2006.

Brookfield, Stephen D. *Developing Critical Thinkers: Challenging Adults to Explore Other Ways of Thinking and Acting.* San Francisco: Jossey-Bass, 1987.

Burkett, Larry. *Budget Counselor Training Course Textbook.* Gainesville, Ga.: Crown Financial Ministries, 2003.

Butler, Phill. *Well Connected: Releasing Power, Restoring Hope Through Kingdom Partnerships.* Colorado Springs: Authentic Publishing, 2005.

Calhoun, Adele A. *Spiritual Disciplines Handbook: Practices That Transform Us.* Downers Grove, Ill.: InterVarsity Press, 2005.

Chen, Yi-feng, Dean Tjosvold and Sofia Fang Su. "Goal Interdependence for Working Across Cultural Boundaries: Chinese Employees with Foreign Managers." *International Journal of Intercultural Relations* 29 (2005): 429-47.

Clark, Carolyn, and Arthur L. Wilson. "Context and Rationality in Mezirow's Theory of Transformational Learning." *Adult Education Quarterly* 41, no. 2 (1991): 75-91.

Collier, Jane. "Conflict Competence Within African, Mexican, and Anglo American Friendships." In *Cross-Cultural Interpersonal Communication*, edited by Stella Ting-Toomey and Felipe Korzenny. Newbury Park, Calif.: Sage, 1991.

Cooperrider, David. Foreword to *Appreciative Inquiry: Change at the Speed of Imagination.* San Francisco: Jossey-Bass/Pfeiffer, 2001.

Cranton, Patricia. "Individual Differences and Transformative Learning." In *Learning as Transformation: Critical Perspectives on a Theory in Progress.* San Franciso: Jossey-Bass, 2000.

———. *Understanding and Promoting Transformative Learning: A Guide for Educators of Adults.* 2nd ed. San Francisco: John Wiley & Sons, 2006.

Da Silva, Anthony, S.J. "Through Nonviolence to Truth: Ghandi's Vision of Reconciliation." In *Forgiveness and Reconciliation*, edited by Raymond G Helmick, S.J., and Rodney L. Peterson. Philadelphia: Templeton Foundation Press, 2001.

Daley, Barbara J. "Learning and Professional Practice: A Study of Four Professions." *Adult Education Quarterly* 52, no. 1 (2001): 39-54.

Daloz, Laurent A. "Transformative Learning for the Common Good." In *Learning as Transformation: Critical Perspectives on a Theory in Progress*. San Franciso: Jossey-Bass, 2000.

Davidheiser, Mark. "Culture and Mediation: A Contemporary Processual Analysis from Southwestern Gambia." *International Journal of Intercultural Relations* 29 (2005): 713-38.

Deutsch, Morton. "Conflicts: Productive and Destructive." In *Conflict Resolution Through Communication*, edited by F. E. Jandt. New York: Harper & Row, 1973.

———. "Conflicts: Productive and Destructive." *Journal of Social Issues* 25 (1969): 7-41.

Dewey, John. *Experience and Education*. New York: Collier, 1938.

Dirkx, John M. "Images, Transformative Learning and the Work of Soul." *Adult Learning* 12, no. 3 (2001): 15-16.

———. "Studying the Complicated Matter of What Works: Evidence-Based Research and the Problem of Practice." *Adult Education Quarterly* 56, no. 4 (2006): 273-90.

Doyle, Charles. "The USA Patriot Act: A Legal Analysis." *CRS Report for Congress*. Washington D.C.: Congressional Research Service: Library of Congress, 2002.

Drever, J. A. *A Dictionary of Psychology*. Harmondsworth, U.K.: Penguin, 1952.

Dubinskas, Frank. "The Cultural Roots of Discord." In *Hidden Conflict in Organizations*, edited by Deborah M. Kolb and Jean M. Bartunek. Newbury Park, Calif.: Sage, 1992.

Duronto, Patricia M., Tsukasa Nishida and Shin-ichi Nakayama. "Uncertainty, Anxiety, and Avoidance in Communication with Strangers." *International Journal of Intercultural Relations* 29 (2005): 549-60.

Earley, P. Christopher, and Elaine Mosakowski. "Cultural Intelligence." *Harvard Business Review* 82, no. 10 (2004): 139-46.

Elmer, Duane. *Cross-Cultural Conflict: Building Relationships for Effective Ministry*. Downers Grove, Ill.: InterVarsity Press, 1993.

————. *Cross-Cultural Connections: Stepping Out and Fitting In Around the World*. Downers Grove, Ill.: InterVarsity Press, 2002.

————. *Cross-Cultural Servanthood: Serving the World in Christlike Humility*. Downers Grove, Ill.: InterVarsity Press, 2006.

Esala, Nathan. "Language Projects and Power Relationships." *Lutheran Bible Translators e-Journal of Mission Studies* 3, no. 1 (2008): 36-42.

Escobar, Samuel. *The New Global Mission: The Gospel from Everywhere to Everywhere*. Downers Grove, Ill.: InterVarsity Press, 2003.

Evangelical Joint Accounting Committee. *Accounting and Financial Reporting Guide for Christian Ministries*. Rev. and exp. Evangelical Joint Accounting Committee, 2001.

Fisher, Roger, and William Ury. *Getting to Yes: Negotiating Agreement Without Giving In*. Middlesex, U.K.: Penguin, 1981.

Fox, Frampton F. "Money as Water: A Patron-Client Approach to Mission Dependency in India." Ph.D. diss., Trinity International University, 2003.

Freire, Paulo. *Pedagogy of the Oppressed*. New York: Continuum, 1970.

Funder, D. C. "Errors and mistakes: Evaluating the Accuracy of Social Judgment." *Psychological Bulletin* 101, no. 1 (1987): 75-90.

Gaebelein, Frank, ed. *The Expositor's Bible Commentary*. Grand Rapids: Regency Reference Library, 1984.

Galford, Robert, and Anne Seibold Drapeau. "The Enemies of Trust." *Harvard Business Review* 81, no. 2 (2003): 88-95.

Gardner, Howard. *Multiple Intelligences*. New York: Basic Books, 1993.

Gibson, DeWan, and Mei Zhong. "Intercultural Communication Competence in the Healthcare Context." *International Journal of Intercultural Relations* 29 (2005) 621-34.

Gilbert, Daniel, and Patrick Malone. "The Correspondence Bias." *Psychological Bulletin* 117, no. 1 (1995): 21-28.

Gilbert, Daniel T., Brett W. Pelham and Douglas S. Krull. "On Cognitive Busyness When Person Perceivers Meet Persons Perceived."

Journal of Personality and Social Psychology 54, no. 5 (1988): 733-40.

Gilkey, Langdon. *Shantung Compound.* New York: HarperCollins, 1966.

Goleman, Daniel. *Emotional Intelligence: Why It Can Matter More Than IQ.* New York: Bantam Books, 1994.

———. *Working with Emotional Intelligence.* New York: Bantam Books, 1998.

Gudykunst, William B. *Bridging Differences: Effective Intergroup Communication.* Newbury Park, Calif.: Sage, 1991.

Gudykunst, William B., and Carmen M. Lee. "Cross-Cultural Communication Theories." In *Cross-Cultural and Intercultural Communication,* edited by William B. Gudykunst. Thousand Oaks, Calif.: Sage, 2003.

Gudykunst, William B., Y. Matsumoto, S. Ting-Toomey, T. Nishida, K. Kim and S. Heyman. "The Influence of Cultural Individualism-Collectivism, Self Construals, and Individual Values on Communication Styles Across Cultures." *Human Communication Research* 22 (1996): 510-43.

Gupta, Paul R., and Sherwood G. Lingenfelter. *Breaking Tradition to Accomplish Vision: Training Leaders for a Church-Planting Movement.* Winona Lake, Ind.: BHM Books, 2006.

Hall, Edward T. *Beyond Culture.* Garden City, N.Y.: Anchor Press, 1976.

———. *The Dance of Life: The Other Dimension of Time.* Garden City, N.Y.: Anchor Press, 1983.

———. *The Hidden Dimension.* Garden City, N.Y.: Anchor Press, 1966.

———. *The Silent Language.* Westport, Conn.: Greenwood Press, 1959.

Hall, Edward T., and Mildred Reed Hall. "The Sounds of Silence." In *Conformity and Conflict: Readings in Cultural Anthropology.* Boston: Little, Brown, 1971.

Hall, J. *Conflict Management Survey: A Survey of One's Characteristic Reaction to and Handling Conflict Between Himself and Others.* Canoe, Tex.: Teleometrics International, 1969.

Hammer, Mitchell R. "The Intercultural Conflict Style Inventory: A Conceptual Framework and Measure of Intercultural Conflict Resolution Approaches." *International Journal of Intercultural Relations* 29 (2005): 675-95.

Hart, Mechthild. "Critical Theory and Beyond: Further Perspectives on Emancipatory Education." *Adult Education Quarterly* 40, no. 3 (1990): 125-38.

Helmick, Raymond G., S.J., and Rodney L. Peterson, eds. *Forgiveness and Reconciliation*. Philadelphia: Templeton Foundation Press, 2001.

Hicks, Donna. "The Role of Identity Reconstruction in Promoting Reconciliation." In *Forgiveness and Reconciliation*, edited by Raymond G. Helmick, S.J., and Rodney L. Peterson. Philadelphia: Templeton Foundation Press, 2001.

Hiebert, Paul G. *Anthropological Insights for Missionaries*. Grand Rapids: Baker Books, 1985.

―――. *Transforming Worldviews*. Grand Rapids: Baker Academic, 2008.

Hiebert, Paul G., and Frances F. Hiebert. *Case Studies in Missions*. Grand Rapids: Baker, 1987.

Ho, D. F. E. "On the Concept of Face." *American Journal of Sociology* 81b (1976): 867-84.

Hofstede, Geert. *Cultures and Organizations: Software of the Mind*. London: McGraw-Hill, 1991.

―――. *Culture's Consequences: International Differences in Work-Related Values*. Beverly Hills: Sage, 1980.

Hofstede, Geert, and Gert Jan Hofstede. *Cultures and Organizations: Software of the Mind*. 2nd ed. New York: McGraw-Hill, 2005.

Holm, Joe. *Church Centered Mission*. United States: Joe Holm Ministry Resources, 2006.

Holt, Jennifer, and Cynthia James DeVore. "Culture, Gender, Organizational Role, and Styles of Conflict Resolution: A Meta-Analysis." *International Journal of Intercultural Relations* 29 (2005): 165-96.

Inkeles, A., and D. J. Levinson. "National Character: The Study of Modal Personality and Sociocultural Systems." In *The Handbook of Social Psychology*, edited by G. Lindzey and E. Aronson, 2nd ed., vol. 4. Reading, Mass.: Addison-Wesley, 1969.

IRS. Tax Information for Churches and Religious Organizations. 2006. Available from http://www.irs.gov/charities/churches/index .htm.

Isaacs, William. *Dialogue and the Art of Thinking Together.* New York: Doubleday, 1999.

Janis, I. L. *Victims of Group Think: A Psychological Study of Foreign-Policy Decisions and Fiascoes.* Boston: Hougton Mifflin, 1972.

Jones, E. E., and R. E. Nisbett. "The Actor and the Observer: Divergent Perceptions of the Causes of Behavior." In Edward E. Jones et al., *Attribution: Perceiving the Causes of Behavior.* Morristown, N.J.: General Learning Press, 1972.

Jussim, Lee, and Kent D. Harber. "Teacher Expectations and Self-Fulfilling Prophesies: Knowns and Unknowns, Resolved and Unresolved Controversies." *Personality and Social Psychology Review* 9, no. 2 (2005): 131-55.

Kealey, Daniel J., David R. Protheroe, Doug MacDonald and Thomas Vulpe. "Re-examining the Role of Training in Contributing to International Project Success: A Literature Review and an Outline of a New Model Training Program. *International Journal of Intercultural Relations* 29 (2005): 289-16.

Kelman, Herbert C. "Building Trust Among Enemies: The Central Challenge for International Conflict Resolution." *International Journal of Intercultural Relations* 29 (2005): 639-50.

Kluckhohn, F. R., and F. L. Strodtbeck. *Variations in Value Orientations.* Evanston, Ill.: Row, Peterson, 1961.

Kolb, Deborah, and Linda L. Putnam. "The Dialectics of Disputing." In *Hidden Conflict in Organizations*, edited by Deborah M. Kolb and Jean M. Bartunek. Newbury Park, Calif.: Sage, 1992.

Larkin, Richard, and Marie DiTommaso. *Not-for-Profit GAAP.* Hoboken, N.J.: John Wiley & Sons, 2004.

Lederach, John Paul. "Five Qualities of Practice in Support of Reconciliation Process." In *Forgiveness and Reconciliation*, edited by Raymond G. Helmick, S.J., and Rodney L. Peterson. Philadelphia: Templeton Foundation Press, 2001.

Lederleitner, Mary. "The Devil Is in the Details: Avoiding Common

Pitfalls When Funding New Partnership Endeavors." *Evangelical Missions Quarterly* 43, no. 2 (2007): 160-65.

———. A Different Approach: Wycliffe's Work in Latin America. How Convictions Can Be Catalytic for Fruitful Cross-Cultural Partnerships." *Evangelical Missions Quarterly,* January 2010.

———."Funding Kingdom Work by Empowering Indigenous Organizations: Lessons Learned in Wycliffe International's Matching Funds Experiment." *Evangelical Missions Quarterly,* July 2009.

———. "Perspective Transformation and Its Application for Church Mission Curriculum." *Common Ground,* March 2008.

———. "The Theology of Internal Controls." *Evangelical Missions Quarterly* 40, no. 4 (2006): 516-21.

Leung, Kwok. "Some Determinants of Conflict Avoidance." *Journal of Cross-Cultural Psychology* 19, no. 1 (1988): 125-36.

Lewis, C. S. *The Weight of Glory.* New York: Touchstone, 1975.

Lingenfelter, Judith E., and Sherwood G. Lingenfelter. *Teaching Cross-Culturally: An Incarnational Model for Learning and Teaching.* Grand Rapids: Baker Academic, 2003.

Lingenfelter, Sherwood G. *Leading Cross-Culturally: Covenant Relationships for Effective Christian Leadership.* Grand Rapids: Baker Academic, 2008.

Lingenfelter, Sherwood G., and Marvin K. Mayers. *Ministering Cross-Culturally: An Incarnational Model for Personal Relationships.* Grand Rapids: Baker Academic, 1986.

Maranz, David. *African Friends and Money Matters.* Dallas: SIL International and the International Museum of Cultures, 2001.

McQuilkin, J. R. "Stop Sending Money: Breaking the Cycle of Missionary Dependency." *Christianity Today,* March 1999, pp. 57-59.

Merriam, Sharan B., and Mozanah Mohamad. "How Cultural Values Shape Learning in Older Adulthood: The Case of Malaysia." *Adult Education Quarterly* 51, no. 1 (2000): 45-63.

Merriam, Sharan B., Rosemary S. Caffarella and Lisa M. Baumgartner. *Learning in Adulthood: A Comprehensive Guide.* 2nd ed. San Francisco: John Wiley & Sons, 2007.

Mezirow, Jack. "Concept and Action in Adult Education." *Adult Education Quarterly* 35, no. 3 (1985): 142-51.

————. *Education for Perspective Transformation: Women's Reentry Programs in Community Colleges.* New York: Center for Adult Education, Teachers College, Columbia University, 1975.

————. Forum comment on Sharan Merriam's "The Role of Cognitive Development in Mezirow's Transformational Learning Theory." *Adult Education Quarterly* 55, no. 1 (2004): 69-70.

————. "Learning to Think Like an Adult: Core Concepts of Transformation Theory." In *Learning as Transformation: Critical Perspectives on a Theory in Progress.* San Fransisco: Jossey-Bass, 2000.

————. "Transformation Theory and Social Action: A Response to Collard and Law." *Adult Education Quarterly* 39, no. 3 (1989): 169-75.

————. "Transformation Theory Out of Context." *Adult Education Quarterly* 48, no. 1 (1997): 60-62.

————. *Transformative Dimensions of Adult Learning.* San Francisco: John Wiley & Sons, 1991.

Miller, D. T., S. A. Norman and E. Wright. "Distortion in Person Perception as a Consequence of the Need for Effective Control." *Journal of Personality and Social Psychology* 36 (1978): 598-607.

Mitchell, Terence, and Stephen Green. "Attribution Theory: Managerial Perceptions of the Poor Performing Subordinate." In John Miner, *Organizational Behavior 1: Essential Theories of Motivation and Leadership.* Armonk, N.Y.: M. E. Sharpe, 2005.

Montville, Joseph V. "Religion and Peacekeeping." In *Forgiveness and Reconciliation,* edited by Raymond G Helmick, S.J., and Rodney L. Peterson. Philadelphia: Templeton Foundation Press, 2001.

Moreau, Scott. "Chapter One." *Mission Handbook 2007-2009.* Wheaton, Ill.: EMIS, 2008.

Morris, Michael W., Katherine Y. Williams, Kwok Leung, Richard Larrick, M. Teresa Mendoza, Deepti Bhatnagar, Jianfeng Li, Mari Kondo, Jin-Lian Luo and Jun-Chen Hu. "Conflict Management Style: Accounting for Cross-National Differences." *Journal of International Business Studies* 29, no. 4 (1998): 729-47.

Morris, Michael W., Kwok Leung and Sheena S. Iyengar. "Person Perceptions in the Heat of Conflict: Negative Trait Attributions Affect Procedureal Preferences and Account for Situational and Cultural Differences." *Asian Journal of Social Psychology* 7, no. 2 (2004): 127-47.

Myers, Bryant L. *Walking with the Poor: Principles and Practices of Transformational Development*. Maryknoll, N.Y.: Orbis, 2007.

Nadler, Lawrence B., Marjorie K. Nadler and Benjamin J. Broome. "Culture and the Management of Conflict Situations. In *Communication, Culture, and Organizational Processes*, edited by William B. Gudykunst, Lea P. Stewart and Stella Ting-Toomey. Beverly Hills: Sage, 1985.

Newman, W. H. "Stages in Cross-Cultural Collaboration." *Journal of Asian Business* 11, no. 4 (1995): 69-95.

Nickerson, Raymond S. "Confirmation Bias: A Ubiquitous Phenomenon in Many Guises." *Review of General Psychology* 2, no. 2 (1998): 175-220.

Nussbaum, Stan. *American Cultural Baggage: How to Recognize and Deal with It*. Maryknoll, N.Y.: Orbis, 2005.

————. *Breakthrough: Steps to Research and Resolve the Mysteries in Your Ministry*. Colorado Springs: GMI Research Services, 2007.

Ortega, Ofelia. "Conversion as a Way of Life in Cultures of Violence." In *Forgiveness and Reconciliation*, edited by Raymond G. Helmick, S.J., and Rodney L. Peterson. Philadelphia: Templeton Foundation Press, 2001.

Parsons, T. *The Social System*. New York: Free Press, 1951.

Parsons, T., and E. A. Shils. *Toward a General Theory of Action*. Cambridge, Mass.: Harvard University Press, 1951.

Perlow, Leslie, and Stephanie Williams. "Is Silence Killing Your Company?" *Harvard Business Review* 81, no. 5 (1951): 52-58.

Peterson, Brooks. 2004. *Cultural Intelligence: A Guide to Working with People from Other Cultures*. Boston: Intercultural Press.

Pettigrew, Thomas F. "The Ultimate Attribution Error: Extending Allport's Cognitive Analysis of Prejudice." *Personality and Social Psychology Bulletin* 5, no. 4 (1975): 461-76.

Piper, John. *Let the Nations Be Glad*. Grand Rapids: Baker Books, 1993.

Pocock, Michael, Gailyn Van Rheenen and Douglas McConnell. *The Changing Face of World Missions: Engaging Contemporary Issues and Trends*. Grand Rapids: Baker Academic, 2005.

Prahalad, C. K., and Kenneth Lieberthal. "The End of Corporate Imperialism." *Harvard Business Review* 81, no. 8 (2003): 109-17.

Putnam, Linda. "Contradictions and Paradoxes in Organizations." In *Organization-Communication: Emerging Perspectives I,* edited by Lee Thayer. Norwood, N.J.: Ablex, 1986.

Rahim, M. A. "A Measure of Styles of Handling Interpersonal Conflict." *Academy of Management Journal* 26, no. 2 (1983): 368-76.

———. *Rahim Organizational Conflict Inventories: Professional Manual.* New York: Consulting Psychologists Press, 1983.

———. "Toward a Theory of Managing Organizational Conflict." *International Journal of Conflict Management* 12, no. 3 (2002): 206-36.

Rahim, M. A., and Albert A. Blum, eds. *Global Perspectives on Organizational Conflict.* Westport, Conn.: Praeger, 1994.

Rickett, Daniel. "Capacity Building. Web Resource for Global Mapping International." 2000. www.gmi.org

———. *Making Your Partnership Work.* Enumclaw, Wash.: WinePress Publishing, 2002.

Rosenthal, Robert. "Interpersonal Expectancy Effects: A 30-Year Perspective." *Current Directions in Psychological Science* 3, no. 6 (1994): 176-79.

———. *On the Social Psychology of the Self-Fulfilling Prophecy: Further Evidence for the Pygmalion Effects.* New York: MSS Modular Publications, 1974.

Rosenthal, Robert, and Lenore Jacobson. *Pygmalion in the Classroom; Teacher Expectation and Pupils' Intellectual Development.* New York: Holt, Rinehart & Winston, 1994.

Rowell, John. *To Give or Not to Give: Rethinking Dependence, Restoring Generosity and Redefining Sustainability.* Atlanta: Authentic Publishing, 2006.

Rubin, J. Z., D. G. Pruitt and S. H. Kim. *Social Conflict.* New York: McGraw-Hill, 1994.

Salzman, Michael. "Attributional Discrepancies and Bias in Cross-Cultural Interactions." *Journal of Multicultural Counseling & Development* 23, no. 3 (1995): 181-93.

Schwartz, Glenn. "Cutting the Apron Strings." *Evangelical Missions Quarterly* 30, no. 1 (1994): 37-42.

―――. *When Charity Destroys Dignity: Overcoming Unhealthy Dependency in the Christian Movement*. Bloomington, Ind.: AuthorHouse, 2007.

Sebenius, James K. "The Hidden Challenge of Cross-Border Negotiations." *Harvard Business Review* 80, no. 3 (2002): 77-85.

Senge, Peter M. *The Fifth Discipline: The Art and Practice of the Learning Organization*. New York: Doubleday, 2006.

―――. Foreword to William Isaacs, *Dialogue and the Art of Thinking Together*. New York: Doubleday, 1999.

Sider, Ronald J. *Rich Christians in an Age of Hunger: Moving from Affluence to Generosity*. Nashville: Thomas Nelson, 2005.

Silverstone, Howard, and Howard R. Davia. *Fraud 101*. 2nd ed. Hoboken, N.J.: John Wiley & Sons, 2005.

Sorenson, R. L., E. A. Morse and G. T. Savage. "A Test of the Motivations Underlying Choice of Conflict Strategies in the Dual-concern Model." *The International Journal of Conflict Management* 10, no. 1 (1999): 25-44.

Stark, Rodney. *The Rise of Christianity*. Princeton, N.J.: Princeton University Press, 1996.

Stephan, Cookie W., and Walter G. Stephan. "Cognition and Affect in Cross-Cultural Relations." In *Cross-Cultural and Intercultural Communication*, edited by William B. Gudykunst. Thousand Oaks, Calif.: Sage, 2003.

Storti, Craig. *Figuring Foreigners Out: A Practical Guide*. Yarmouth, Me.: Intercultural Press, 1999.

Struch, N., and S. H. Struch. "Intergroup Aggression: Its Predictors and Distinctness from In-Group Bias." *Journal of Personality and Social Psychology* 56, no. 3 (1989): 364-73.

Tafoya, Dennis. "The Roots of Conflict: A Theory of Typology." In *Intercultural Communication Theory*, edited by William B. Gudykunst. Newbury Park, Calif.: Sage, 1983.

Tan, Kang-San. "Who Is in the Driver's Seat? A Critique of Mission Partnership Models Between Western Missions and East Asian Mission Movements." *Encounters Mission Ezine* 24, June 2008.

Tarr, Noreen D., Mind-Sun Kim and William F. Sharkey. "The Effects of Self-Construals and Embarrassability on Predicament Response

Strategies." *International Journal of Intercultural Relations* 29 (2005): 497-520.

Taylor, Edward W. "Analyzing Research on Transformative Learning Theory." In Jack Mezirow and Associates, *Learning as Transformation: Critical Perspectives on a Theory in Progress*. San Franciso: Jossey-Bass 2000.

————. "Intercultural Competency: A Transformative Learning Process." *Adult Education Quarterly* 44, no. 3 (1994): 154-74.

————. "Transformative Learning Theory: A Neurobiological Perspective of the Role of Emotions and Unconscious Ways of Knowing." *International Journal of Lifelong Education* 220, no. 3 (2001): 218-36.

Tetlock, Philip E. "Accountability: A Social Check on the Fundamental Attribution Error." *Social Psychology Quarterly* 48, no. 3 (1985): 227-36.

Thomas, K. W., and R. H. Kilmann. *Thomas-Kilmann Conflict Mode Instrument*. Tuxedo, N. Y.: Xicom, 1974.

Ting-Toomey, Stella. *Communicating Across Cultures*. New York: Guilford, 1999.

————. "A Face Negotiation Theory." In *Theories in Intercultural Communication*, edited by Y. Kim and William B. Gudykunst. Newbury Park, Calif.: Sage, 1988.

————. "Toward a Theory of Conflict and Culture." In *Communication, Culture, and Organizational Processes*, edited by William B. Gudykunst, Lea P. Stewart and Stella Ting-Toomey. Beverly Hills: Sage, 1985.

Ting-Toomey, Stella, and John G. Oetzel. "Cross-Cultural Face Concerns and Conflict Styles. In *Cross-Cultural and Intercultural Communication*, edited by William B. Gudykunst. Thousand Oaks, Calif.: Sage, 2003.

Ting-Toomey, Stella, G. Gao, P. Trubinsky, Z. Yang, H. S. Kim, S. L. Lin and T. Nishida. "Culture, Face Maintenance, and Styles of Handling Interpersonal Conflict: A Study in Five Cultures." *International Journal of Conflict Management* 2, no. 2 (1991): 275-96.

Ting-Toomey, Stella, K. K. Yee-Jung, R. B. Shapiro, W. Garcia, T. J. Wright and J. G. Oetzel. "Ethnic/Cultural Identity Salience and

Conflict Styles in Four US Ethnic Groups." *International Journal of Intercultural Relations* 24 (2000): 47-81.

Tisdell, Elizabeth J., and Denise E. Tolliver. "The Role of Spirituality in Culturally Relevant and Transformative Adult Education." *Adult Learning* 12, no. 3 (2001): 3-14.

Triandis, Harry. "Collectivism vs. Individualism: A Reconceptualization of a Basic Concept in Cross-Cultural Psychology." In *Cross-Cultural Studies of Personality, Attitudes and Cognition,* edited by G. Verma and C. Bagley. London: Macmillan, 1988.

———. "Individualism-Collectivism and Personality." *Journal of Personality* 69, no. 6 (2001): 907-24.

Trompenaars, Fons, and Charles Hampden-Turner. *Riding the Waves of Culture: Understanding Diversity in Global Business.* 2nd ed. New York: McGraw-Hill, 1998.

Trubisky, P., S. Ting-Toomey and S. L. Lin. "The Influence of Individualism: Collectivism and Self Monitoring on Conflict Styles." *International Journal of Intercultural Relations* 15, no. 1 (1991): 65-84.

Van Cleef, Carol R. "The USA Patriot Act: Statutory Analysis and Regulatory Implementation." *Journal of Financial Crime* 11, no. 1 (2003): 73-102.

Van de Vliert, E., and Boris Kabanoff. "Toward Theory-Based Measures of Conflict Management." *Academy of Management Journal* 33, no. 1 (1990): 199-209.

Vella, Jan. *Taking Learning to Task: Creative Strategies for Teaching Adults.* San Franciso: John Wiley & Sons, 2001.

Vygotsky, L. S. *Mind in Society.* Cambridge, Mass.: Harvard University Press, 1978.

Watkins, Jane M., and Bernard J. Mohr. *Appreciative Inquiry: Change at the Speed of Imagination.* San Francisco: Jossey-Bass/Pfeiffer, 2001.

Weeks, Holly. "Taking the Stress Out of Stressful Conversations." *Harvard Business Review* 79, no. 7 (2001): 112-19.

Weiss, Jeff, and Jonathan Hughes. "Want Collaboration? Accept and Actively Manage Conflict." *Harvard Business Review* 83, no. 3 (2005): 92-101.

Whitney, Diana, and Amanda Trosten-Bloom. *The Power of Appreciative Inquiry: A Practical Guide to Positive Change*. San Francisco: Berrett-Koehler, 2003.

Wiessner, Collen A., Jack Mezirow and Cheryl A. Smith. "Theory Building and the Search for Common Ground." In Jack Mezirow and Associates, *Learning as Transformation: Critical Perspectives on a Theory in Progress*. San Francisco: Jossey-Bass, 2000.

Willmer, Wesley K. *God and Your Stuff: The Vital Link Between Your Possessions and Your Soul*. Colorado Springs: NavPress, 2002.

Wilson, Myles. *Funding the Family Business: A Handbook for Raising Personal Support*. Essex, U.K.: Stewardship, 2006.

Wiseman, Richard L. "Intercultural Communication Competence." In *Cross-Cultural and Intercultural Communication*, edited by William B. Gudykunst. Thousand Oaks, Calif.: Sage, 2003.

Wlodkowski, Raymond J. *Enhancing Adult Motivation to Learn: A Comprehensive Guide for Teaching All Adults*. San Francisco: Jossey-Bass, 1999.

Wood, Ed, and Les Willis. "Paternalism, Accountability, Responsibility and Transparency." IMCO Conference. Saskatchewan, Canada, 2007.

Worchel, Stephen. "Culture's Role in Conflict and Conflict Management: Some Suggestions, Many Questions." *International Journal of Intercultural Relations* 29 (2005): 739-57.

Yohannan, K. P. *Revolution in World Missions*. Carrolton, Tex.: GFA Books, 2004.

ABOUT THE AUTHOR

Mary Lederleitner is a researcher, author, trainer and consultant for Wycliffe International. Currently her focus is best practices related to cross-cultural ministry partnerships. She also develops resources to train missionaries and laypeople for more effective cross-cultural ministry. Prior to serving in this role she was the Asia Area Finance Manager and Head of International Audit. She has traveled extensively overseas and has been called on to assist a wide range of Christian nonprofit ministries and churches. Before joining Wycliffe she served as a singles ministry coordinator at College Hill Presbyterian Church (Cincinnati, Ohio) and Christ Church of Oak Brook (Oak Brook, Illinois), equipping laypeople for ministry within the church and the surrounding community. Before entering ministry she became a Certified Public Accountant, and she served as a tax examiner for the Internal Revenue Service and the city of Cincinnati. She is pursuing a Ph.D. in educational studies at Trinity Evangelical Divinity School, and she holds a master's degree in intercultural studies from Wheaton College Graduate School. She is on the advisory board for EMIS, the organization that publishes (*Evangelical Missions Quarterly (EMQ)* and *Lausanne World Pulse*. She also serves on the board of Faith and Learning and the steering committee for the Coalition on the Support of Indigenous Ministries (COSIM) and Mission Leadership Network (MLN). She can be reached by e-mail at mary_lederleitner@wycliffe.net